Nobody's Better Than You,

Mom

ISBN: 978-0-88290-817-5

Published by Horizon, an imprint of Cedar Fort, Inc., 2373 W. 700 S., Springville, UT, 84663
Distributed by Cedar Fort, Inc. www.cedarfort.com

LIBRARY OF CONGRESS CATALOGING-IN-PUBLICATION DATA

Bowen, Debbie, 1962-
  Nobody's better than you, Mom / Debbie Bowen.
    p. cm.
  ISBN 978-0-88290-817-5 (acid-free paper)
  1. Motherhood--Literary collections. I. Title.
  PS3602.O8955N63 2007
  810.8'035252--dc22

                          2006101435

Cover design by Nicole Williams
Edited and typeset by Annaliese B. Cox
Cover design © 2006 by Lyle Mortimer

Printed in the United States of America

10 9 8 7 6 5 4 3 2 1

Printed on acid-free paper

Nobody's Better Than You, Mom

Mom

Debbie Bowen

Horizon Publishers
Springville, Utah

Dedication

To my children
Trenton, Jadee, Caleb, Camille, Isaac,
Jarom, Abram, Levi, Melia, and Marissa

Table of Contents

MOTHERS

Mothers are people who cook things
Like breakfast or lunch or a snack;
Dexterous people who hook things
Which button or zip up the back.
Mothers are people who blow things,
Balloons and kisses and noses;
Green-thumbish people who grow things
Like ivy and puppies and roses.
Mothers are people who send things
Like letters and strawberry tarts;
Magical people who mend things
Like blue jeans and elbows and hearts.
Mothers are people who find things
Like mittens and homework and germs;
Fussbudget people who mind things
Like cusswords and snowballs and worms.
Mothers are people who sweep things
Like porches and cobwebs and rugs.
Softhearted people who keep things
Like artwork, report cards, and hugs.
Mothers are people who nurse things,
A boy or a girl or a spouse.
And all in all there are worse things
Than mothers to have in your house.

—AUTHOR UNKNOWN[1]

MOTHERHOOD IS . . .

The purest joy the heart can feel,
The strongest bond that love can seal,
The deepest truth that life can teach,
The greatest height the soul can reach.

—FLORA S. HORNE[2]

Two and a Half

Hold him a little longer,
Rock him a little more.
Tell him another story
(You've only told him four).
Let him sleep on your shoulder,
Rejoice in his happy smile.
He is only two and a half
For such a little while!

—Author Unknown[4]

On Being a Mother

There's a lot that goes into mothering
So much I didn't see.
But now I can understand,
Because now that mother is me.
It begins with a precious baby,
Straight from Heaven above.
Sent for me to take care of,
To hold, to teach, and to love.
It starts out rather slowly—
Without knowing what's in store,
And then without even realizing,
We get ourselves into more.
So many hours of cooking and cleaning and caring,
Endless efforts of every kind.
But mothers are all about sharing,
I guess that's why we don't mind.
Then over the years and over the miles
Through good and bad, pleasure and sorrow—
Occasional rewards and endless trials,
We must never forget, there's always tomorrow.
So, until you have actually been one,
You can never quite relate;
But now that I have become one,
I can really appreciate.
It takes a special person to be a mother;
The best is hard to find.
Their love is like no other—
The enduring, eternal kind.
And this love can't be measured;
It comes from the heart and the soul—
Each memory sacredly treasured
In pursuing their motherly role.

—LORIE R. BUTTERFIELD[3]

Mom, You're the One

Her children arise up, and call her blessed.

For Christmas one year, my three-year-old son received a small, plastic dart gun with suction-tipped darts. He was thrilled with the gift, and as soon as the presents were opened, he commenced target practice. It wasn't long before he discovered a small ledge by the stairs on which he could line up little Lincoln Logs to shoot. His first shots were awkward and far from the mark. After watching his vain attempts for several minutes, I left the room to do other things. A short time later, he came running down the hall exclaiming excitedly, "Mom . . . Mom, did you see that?"

"No," I replied regretfully.

"Well," he pouted, "I wanted you to be there."

When viewed through grown-up eyes, it was such a simple thing—a small, plastic gun and a handful of Lincoln Logs, but to my son at that moment, it was everything. It was adventure and achievement, excitement and ecstasy. It was a moment of victory, and he wanted me to be there to share it with him.

The disappointment on his face lingered in my mind and his words echoed repeatedly, "I wanted you to be there . . . I wanted you to be there . . . I wanted you to be there." Since then I have wondered how many times my children have silently wished that I had been there for them. I found myself wondering, *Am I making myself available to my children? Am I there to share their excitement, their frustrations, their joys and their sorrows? Am I there for the major events of their lives and even the not so major but still just as important events of their lives? Do they know that I am genuinely interested in their daily struggles and challenges? Do they know that I care about the little things—a Lego creation, a tea party, a snowman, a hut made from couch cushions, a book they've read, a song they've played, a movie they've seen, a thought, a new friend, a school essay, a date, a job . . . or even a direct hit from a small, plastic dart gun?*

On another occasion, this same little three-year-old came bounding into my room to ask if I would zip and button his pants. I was preoccupied at the time, and, a bit annoyed, I suggested, "Isn't there someone else who could help you with that?"

"No!" he responded promptly and resolutely.

Since he was the sixth child in our family, I knew there were others available, so I insisted, "Yes, there is. There's Daddy and Trenton and Jadee . . . " and I named everyone in the family who could help him.

He listened politely, and when I finished, he looked directly at me and said quite matter-of-factly, "Mom, you're the one." A house full of people, and he chose me! What a compliment. . . . What a privilege. . . . What a responsibility!

My heart was touched, and I stooped to button his little-boy pants. He promptly ran off to play without giving the incident a second thought, but his words struck my heart. In his own special way he had preached a powerful sermon as he summed up the role of motherhood in just a few simple words.

Mom, you're the one who can soothe and quiet the crying baby. You're the one who can kiss a scratch and take away all the pain. You're the one a child wants when he wakes up sick or scared during the night. You're the one a child turns to when she has a talk to give, a project to prepare, or an essay to write; you're the one she looks for in the crowd at a soccer game, a recital, or the school play. You're the one who helps with Cub Scouts, Little League, and dance lessons. You're the one who insists that a child practice the piano every day. You're the one who reminds the children to brush their teeth, make their beds, and hang up their clothes. You're the one who is there to share the anticipation and the excitement of that first day of school, and you're the one who is there to share their tears of frustration and rejection. You're the one who remembers birthdays, holidays, and baseball practice. In short, Mom, you're the motivating force behind much that is good in their lives.

One day my children filled their kiddie pool and were eagerly anticipating some carefree, boisterous romping and splashing. Seven of them were planning to swim, from the thirteen-year-old down to the two-year-old. As they were darting through the house grabbing swimsuits, towels, and other necessary items, five-year-old Isaac asked if I would like to swim. I really didn't want to, and I had a dozen reasons why I couldn't. However, the sparkle in his eyes, the anticipation on his hopeful face, and the pleading in his voice told me there was only one correct answer. "Okay," I relented amidst cheers of glee and triumph.

I must admit, I felt ridiculous and awkward in the miniature pool, but the children didn't seem to notice. There were shouts of, "Look, Mommy!" and "Watch me!" and "Look at this!" Everyone thirsted for my attention as if this were the first time they had ever been in the pool. Then suddenly it dawned on me—while this was certainly not *their* first time in this pool, it was the first time *I* had been in it with them. What a rare opportunity, and they were intent on making the most of it. It didn't take long for the noise level to crescendo and the splashing to become more vigorous, and I decided it was time for me to get out. Of course, the children protested when I told them this, and seven-year-old Camille pricked my conscience by saying, "No, Mom, it's more fun with you!"

Could it be said more sincerely? As mothers, we occupy a unique and cherished spot in the hearts of our children. We must not underestimate the power of our position.

To bear and nurture children is our blessing and privilege. We must give this most irreplaceable work our greatest effort. We must make time to "be there" for our children. How true it is that the hand that rocks the cradle rules the world. Many can try and some will come close, but no one can fill the role of mother quite like mother.

My little son emphasized this point during an extended illness in which he lay sick on the couch, burning up with fever. Although he slept most of the time, he woke occasionally for brief periods, stretching out his little arms and calling in a weak voice, "Mama, I want you." Whenever he did this, I picked him up, hugged him tenderly for a moment, and calmed him by saying, "I want you, too." That was all it took—a brief moment of my time and a few loving words—and he was again fast asleep. It was during one of these rocking/cuddling sessions that he passionately proclaimed with all the sincerity of a four-year-old, "Nobody in the who-o-ole world is better than you. *Nobody's* better than you, Mom!"

I took a deep breath and sat a little taller in the chair. I was somebody special! I had, from time to time, considered myself a nobody of sorts, but not quite in this way. He had just put a whole new twist on my self-concept. Suddenly I was a nobody who was somebody—and not just anybody. I was somebody who was better than *everybody*. Now that was somebody indeed!

Compared to all the important and influential people of the world, I had naively and mistakenly viewed my role in the grand scheme of things as having little consequence. Now my little son was telling me that nobody in the world was better than me. Wow! What a declaration.

If I had ever wondered about my role as mother, there was no doubt about it now. I knew there was nothing I might be doing that was more important—no vacation, no social engagement, no charitable cause, no promotion at work. All too soon he would be too big and too grown-up to sit on my lap and snuggle in a chair. Right now, however, it was my privilege to hold and cuddle and comfort him. At this tender age, I could provide a sense of safety and security that would sustain him through the difficult years that would surely follow.

Despite this understanding of the significance of motherhood, I never realized how demanding and discouraging it could be. My own mother seemed to glide effortlessly through her mothering tasks. She worked from dawn to dusk day after day without complaint and made motherhood look so easy and uncomplicated. It wasn't until I had children of my own that I learned the truth.

Over the years I have found that motherhood is much more than the happy fantasy I envisioned while playing dolls as a child. Somehow in my young mind I never imagined the stress, hard work, fatigue, and emotional drain involved in being a mother, nor could I have ever imagined the personal growth and strength of character that I would develop from those challenges. I guess I would say that motherhood has been the most terribly wonderful undertaking of my life.

This book is for mothers everywhere. While it contains my own perspectives and experiences—which may be different from yours—it is my hope that through the common thread of motherhood, you will find some comfort, some encouragement, and some inspiration to fortify you against the onslaught of daily challenges. I share your joys and your sorrows, your happiness and your grief, your simple pleasures and your bitter tears. Through good times and bad, may you always remember that "you're the one." Nobody in the whole world is better than you. *Nobody's* better than you, Mom!

Notes

1 Jack Lyon, ed., *Best-Loved Poems of the LDS People* (Salt Lake City: Deseret Book, 1996), 221.

2 Ibid., 224.

3 Used with permission.

4 Lyon, ed., *Best-Loved Poems*, 24.

BACKWARD

Backward, turn backward, O Time, in your flight,
Make me a child again just for tonight!
Mother, come back from the echoless shore,
Take me again to your heart, as of yore;
Kiss from my forehead the furrows of care,
Smooth the few silver threads out of my hair;
Over my slumbers your loving watch keep,
Rock me to sleep, Mother, rock me to sleep.

—ELIZABETH AKERS ALLEN[1]

THE SUPERGLUE OF LIFE

Mother's arms are made of tenderness,
and sweet sleep blesses the child who lies therein.

—VICTOR HUGO

*T*oday was payday, although I didn't know it when I woke up this morning. Most of the day was pretty routine, but when I pulled back the covers in preparation for bed, I was surprised to find two miniature Reese's peanut butter cups on my pillow along with a note from my thirteen-year-old son. The note said, "Thanks for being the best mom and dad. Love, Isaac."

How sweet. This was certainly a parental payday—a token reward for all our efforts. These small, sporadic payments make all the sacrifice and stress worthwhile. It's what we live for as parents. As I read the note, a tear dropped unexpectedly onto the paper.

Then from somewhere deep inside, something came screaming out of me, *It's not true! It's not true! A good mother—maybe—on a good day, but certainly not "the best mom." There are mothers far more patient than you, mothers more tolerant and loving, more understanding. You jump to conclusions. You're often too busy to really listen. And you lost your cool with him just the other day. What's more, this is the very same son who has threatened to run away on more than one occasion. How does that make you a good parent? It simply is not true!* Another tear fell onto the paper.

Feeling certain that I did not qualify for such an exalted tribute, I was about to march into his room, throwing back the note with shame and humiliation, when other thoughts pushed their way to the front of my consciousness. *Well . . . you certainly aren't perfect, but you are trying; and you must have succeeded more than you've failed or he would have never written the note. Despite your shortcomings, you have somehow, sometime made him feel special, and the thoughts that came sifting back to him tonight are ones of acceptance and love. That has to count for something.*

Okay, I conceded, *perhaps you are right. Thank goodness our children's love does not depend upon our perfection. Thank goodness children love us in spite of ourselves. But then, it's only fair,* I reasoned. *After all, don't we likewise love them in much the same way?*

At that moment I decided that if we could both have these feelings of love *most* of the time, we were on the right track. Besides, there had been times when I too had thought about running away—but not tonight. Tonight I was the "best mom," and I resolved to try a little harder to make it so.

On another occasion, I walked hand-in-hand to the grocery store with my little blond-haired, curly-headed four-year-old son, chatting casually, not really discussing anything in particular, just delighting in each other's company. His hands were so small, his eyes so bright and full of excitement; I wondered if he knew how much I loved him. Then, unexpectedly he declared, "Mom, when I grow up I'm going to marry you!"

Now that's a pretty strong attraction! I was sure he wouldn't always feel that way. In fact, someday he may not even like me. But on that day, I was thrilled with the idea of being loved by my little one, and I was determined to do my best to promote those feelings as long as possible.

Years ago as I sat reading to my children from the book *Where the Wild Things Are*, I came to a point in the story where the little boy was lonely and sad and "wanted to be where someone loved him best of all." At this point I stopped and looked at my children and said, "Who loves *you* best of all?"

Without any hesitation, my four-year-old son pointed to me and exclaimed, "You!" At this young age, he already sensed the deep and unfailing love that I had for him. Despite his mischievousness and disobedience, despite the work and stress and effort, I still loved him. No matter what he did or was or looked like, I loved him. I was, after all, his mother. A mother's love transcends status or stature or standing; it transcends time and space. I believe it even transcends mortality and continues on through eternity.

Love is a feeling that has no words. It is the deepest, most delicate stirrings of the soul. It is the first lesson of motherhood. What confidence God must have to entrust us with His precious little ones. Their innocence and frailty touch our tender motherly affections in a most reverent way.

I remember lying in the hospital with my first child shortly after he was born, carefully studying every feature of his tiny face. I thought he was so perfect, and I marveled at the miracle that he was. Each child since has brought just as much love and wonder. In fact, I think I cherished each successive baby a little more as I realized what a priceless, short-lived treasure a baby really is.

We have all heard the question, "Which came first—the chicken or the egg?" My question regarding motherhood is, "Which comes first— the love or the sacrifice?" Do we sacrifice for our children because we love them or does the sacrifice create the love? I think I learned the answer by watching animal babies.

In past years our family has owned dairy goats, and we have stood marveling at the process of birth. First one baby, then two, sometimes three, and once as many as four baby goats from the same mother! These were exciting, magical moments for us as we watched the limp, scrawny newborns attempt to stand on knobby, skinny legs that could scarcely hold them just moments after birth.

At times, especially at the end of a stressful day with a cranky baby, I have wondered why human babies don't learn to eat and walk immediately after birth like animal babies do. But over the years, I have come to understand an important principle: We learn to love those for whom we sacrifice. There is something about the unending sacrifice and service we give our children that creates the fierce, enduring love we feel for them. Someone said that "it is by loving and not by being loved that one can come nearest to the soul of another."[2]

A few years ago, we were having some challenges with one of our children. We struggled with the situation, wondering how to best handle it. Again and again the thought came to me, *Just love her; just love her.* What?! No new theory, no complicated formula, no special child therapy . . . just plain, simple, genuine love? What a novel idea! I wonder if this might not be the answer to many of the problems we face with our children. I believe that nonjudgmental, unconditional, sincere acceptance of another can do more for their emotional well-being than anything else. Love them first, last, and in between—especially when they don't deserve it, for that is when they need it most of all.

I am reminded of a book I bought for my children years ago. It tells the story of a mother as she watches her son grow from birth to manhood, describing the challenges of each phase of his life. At the end of each stressful day, the mother would creep into her son's room while he was sleeping, pick him up, and rock him back and forth while she sang:

I'll love you forever,
I'll like you for always,
As long as I'm living
My baby you'll be.[3]

There is something precious about sleeping children. In their sleep, they somehow magically transform into the angels we wish they were. Tears come easily as I wander from room to room, pausing a moment at each bedside to reflect on the positive qualities of each child. Somehow the cares of the day—the sloppily made bed, the clothes on the floor, the spilled orange juice, the angry words, the crying, the arguing, the unfinished homework, the dirty dishes, the last-minute errands, the chaos and commotion—all seem to dissipate as I listen to their quiet, steady breathing.

What was so overwhelming only hours ago is now replaced by tender memories—the daily ritual of snuggling with my three-year-old as soon as he awoke to ensure that his day got off to a good start; a quick "thanks for breakfast" as my children leave for school; a phone call from my oldest to inform me of the latest progress with his class schedule change; a spontaneous, heartfelt hug from a toddler; stories, books, and games with the little ones; reading with my first grader; my two-year-old running down the hall towards my outstretched arms at the end of his nap; a leisurely visit with my children at the end of the school day; completion of a school project; a task well-done without any nagging on my part; my daughter bathing the little ones without being asked; a thank you note on my pillow; the sincere, simple prayer of a three-year-old; a kiss on the cheek and a soft "I love you" as I tuck them into bed.

A mother's love runs deep, and children do best on large doses of this love dispensed frequently. When my son Abram was three, he insisted on sitting in a chair and snuggling every morning as soon as he was up. One morning I was particularly busy and overlooked this important event. I soon noticed, however, that he was looking rather grumpy, and I questioned him about it. In his most pouty voice, he replied dejectedly, "You didn't snuggle with me." Immediately, I left what I was doing, gathered him up in my arms, and proceeded to rock him back and forth for several minutes. Soon enough he was happy and jumped off my lap ready to start the day. The change in his countenance was amazing, and I wondered about the power of a mother's love.

One son beautifully summarized the power of his mother's love:

> I don't remember much about her views on voting nor her social prestige; and what her ideas on child training, diet, and eugenics were, I cannot recall. The main thing that sifts back to me now through the thick undergrowth of years is that she loved me. She liked to lie on the grass with me and tell stories, or to run and hide with us children. She was always hugging me. And I liked it. She had a sunny face. To me it was like God, and all the beatitudes saints tell of Him. And sing! Of all the sensations pleasurable to my life nothing can compare with the rapture of crawling up into her lap and going to sleep while she swung to and fro in her rocking chair and sang. Thinking of this, I wonder if the woman of today, with all her tremendous notions and plans, realizes what an almighty factor she is in shaping of her child for weal or woe. I wonder if she realizes how much sheer love and attention count for in a child's life.[4]

Mothers come in all shapes and sizes, each uniquely matched for the children that are hers. Little children don't care and probably don't even notice if their mother's hair has been newly permed and cut and curled in the latest style. They don't care if her makeup is fresh and beautiful or if she's even wearing any at all. It doesn't matter if mother is thin or heavy, short or tall, brilliant or uneducated. They don't know, nor do they care, what degrees or titles she may have earned or how many awards and honors she may have been given. What they do know, however, and all they really care about is that you are their mother. More than anything, they want your genuine love and attention.

Loving and cuddling and serving come naturally to mothers. With our nurturing natures, we are uniquely qualified to provide the special love for which children yearn and on which they thrive. Despite our imperfections, we are still the best thing God has for raising happy, well-adjusted children.

> Motherhood is the greatest potential influence either for good or ill in human life. The mother's image is the first that stamps itself on the unwritten page of the young child's mind. It is her caress that first awakens a sense of security; her kiss, the first realization of affection; her sympathy and tenderness, the first assurance that there is love in the world. This ability and willingness properly to rear children, the gift to love, and eagerness, yes, longing to express it in soul development, make motherhood the noblest office or calling in the world.[5]

Too often we feel guilt for all the things we aren't or can't or shouldn't be. We beat ourselves up over being short on patience and long on lectures, in a hurry and out of sorts. It happens to all of us from time to time. Thank goodness children are forgiving people. Thank goodness they love us because of who we are, not who we aren't. Remember, children don't love us because we're perfect. They love us because we first loved them and because they recognize our daily strivings in their behalf.

Do not confuse the titles "best mom" with "perfect mom." The "best mom" acknowledges her mistakes, resolves to do better, and moves forward with renewed determination. No one could ask for more. As inadequate as you may sometimes feel, never forget that nobody's better at loving *your* children than you, Mom.

Notes

1 Lyon, ed., *Best-Loved Poems*, 226.

2 George McDonald, quoted by Spencer W. Kimball, "The Abundant Life," *Ensign*, July 1978, 3.

3 Robert Munsch, *Love You Forever* (Buffalo, NY: Firefly Books, Inc., 1998).

4 Ezra Taft Benson, "To the Mothers in Zion," Fireside Address given 22 February 1987 (The Church of Jesus Christ of Latter-day Saints, 1987), 1.

5 David O. McKay, *Gospel Ideals* (Salt Lake City: Improvement Era, 1953), 452–54.

I Have Wept in the Night

I have wept in the night
For the shortness of sight
That to somebody's need made me blind;
But I never have yet
Felt a tinge of regret
For being a little too kind.

—AUTHOR UNKNOWN[1]

"Go feed the hungry sweet charity's bread.
"For giving is living," the angel said.
"And must I keep giving and giving again?"
My selfish and querulous question ran.
"Oh no," said the angel, his eyes pierced me through.
"Just give till the Master stops giving to you."

—AUTHOR UNKNOWN

Service

A Powerful Tonic

By love serve one another.

—Galatians 5:13

*D*o good intentions count for service? If so, I deserve an A. If not, I'm afraid I have not done so well.

I can't tell you how many times I've *thought* about making cookies or bread or dinner for someone else or how many times I've *thought* about stopping by or making a phone call. Even worse, I can't tell you how many plates of cookies I have baked intending to do a good deed for a neighbor, but for some reason or other, they never reach their intended destination. At times I have actually made the effort to stop by, only to find no one home. *I'll come again tomorrow,* I tell myself, *when I take the kids to piano lessons.* But tomorrow I am halfway to piano before I remember about the cookies. *Oh well, I'll do it some other time,* I think with smug assurance; but somehow that "other time" never happens.

Days later, I find the cookies carefully tucked away in some obscure cupboard so the children won't get to them. But now they are too stale to deliver without dramatically diminishing the intended goodwill and any sort of culinary reputation I may have had. My children, oblivious to their outdated condition, hungrily gobble them up while I am left feeling slothful and negligent.

Good deeds do not usually come easily and are most often not convenient. Nevertheless, by reaching out to those around us, we experience a connectedness with our fellowman that can be achieved in no other way. Where we might otherwise find loneliness and despair, service provides purpose and meaning to our lives as we focus less on ourselves and more on others.

> Service to others deepens and sweetens this life while we are preparing to live in a better world. It is by serving that we learn how to serve. When we are engaged in the service of our fellowmen, not only do our deeds assist them, but we put our own problems in a fresher perspective. When we concern ourselves more with others, there is less time to be concerned with ourselves! In the midst of the miracle of serving, there is the promise . . . that by losing ourselves, we find ourselves![2]

With the birth of my third baby came a profound lesson on the healing power of service. Not only was this baby more difficult than the previous two had been, but I also had some health problems which complicated life even more. In addition, my husband's work and school schedule required the use of our only vehicle, leaving me home all day with the children. The daily grind of caring for three children under the age of four was not a pleasant task. I found myself feeling tired, lonely, and trapped.

I had often heard it said by those much wiser than I that by serving others we heal ourselves. In desperation, I decided to try an experiment to test the validity of their words. Selfishly, at first, I began reaching out to others. Loading my children in our little red wagon, I delivered bread, cookies, and meals to neighbors. I visited a lonely grandmother.

I also learned that I could have an effect on others without even leaving home. I wrote words of encouragement to friends and family and sent letters to senators and congressmen on issues that affected me. I made small donations to worthy charitable groups.

Those little deeds of service began to grow into something wonderful. From the crucible of personal experience, I came to know that service is indeed a true principle. In the midst of losing myself in the service of others, I truly found myself. I found my own capacity enlarged, my patience increased, and my joy more full. What a miracle!

Looking back, I should have learned this lesson long ago. My own mother, a superb cook, was an excellent example of service. We children often returned home to find tasty treats cooling on the counter. However, we never casually assumed that we would be the beneficiaries of my mother's efforts. Instead, we always asked warily (and sometimes a bit angrily), "Is this for us?" At an early age, we were taught to sacrifice our own wants for the needs of others.

Regrettably, it took some time for this lesson to sink in. Nevertheless, years later, as I began to focus on the needs of others instead of wallowing in self-pity, my own problems began to dwindle in significance. I began to grow outside myself as I viewed life with a broader perspective than merely the four walls of my own home. Not only did I see others with equally difficult challenges, but I also became aware of larger, more complex issues in society that made me grateful to be home where I could nurture my little ones and give them a solid foundation to prepare them for the challenges of life. Each time I did a kind deed for someone, I felt greater peace, which yielded wonderful results for myself and my family. I was better able to eliminate gloominess and replace it with gladness.

I remember one time specifically when I had prepared dinner for an elderly neighbor. Everything was ready to deliver as soon as my husband came home. My plan was to drop the food off and hurry home so we could enjoy our own dinner while it was still warm. However, the neighbor invited us in, and, as elderly people tend to do, he proudly began showing us the many pictures and treasures he had accumulated over the years. After visiting for some time, we returned home to our own now-cold dinner.

As I reheated the food, however, I noticed that something was different. Whereas I would normally have been tense and uptight trying to get everything on the table at just the right moment, I felt unusually calm and peaceful, and I was more patient with the children. Although the food was no longer at its peak, it didn't seem to matter. One layer of stress had peeled away, and I marveled at the impact of service on my own attitude. I had intended to brighten someone else's day, but instead I found my own world a little brighter.

Time and time again, I have felt the magical load-lightening, soul-lifting influence of service in my own life. Never do I feel so worthwhile as when I am doing something nice for someone else. It was a wonderful experiment, and I highly recommend it for anyone feeling lonely, depressed, or discouraged. In the process of giving, we also receive, and the more we give, the more we receive. What a wonderful cycle.

My children are also learning this cycle of giving. When we moved to Hawaii—3,500 miles from home and family—we felt a loss and an emptiness. However, one woman at church who was old enough to be my children's grandmother began sitting on our bench, initiating an exciting adventure of sharing and receiving. My two little boys, ages four and five, liked sitting next to her while they drew pictures or looked at storybooks. They enjoyed telling her the news from the preceding week or the anticipated events of the week to come. They colored pictures during the week to give to her the following Sunday. And while I think we made her world a little brighter since her own grandchildren were also far away, her association with us was rewarding and enriching and helped fill a void in our own lives. Years after leaving Hawaii, she is still our Granny, and we keep in touch through letters and phone calls, and even surprise visits from her—all the way from Hawaii! Once again, the giving cycle is complete.

I know life can get pretty crazy at times—running here and chasing there. We have a half dozen more things to do in a day than prudently possible for one mother to accomplish. We have more stress than medically acceptable to prevent serious illness and severe cases of insanity. Fortunately, mothers can survive in a near comatose state. Sometimes I think we do better that way—then we don't realize just how bad it really is! We're all busier than anyone else—or at least it seems that way—and, yet, if we could hop off the merry-go-round for just a moment, we would most likely find someone who is more busy, more stressed, more lonely, more sick, or more tired.

Appearances can be deceiving. Just because others *seem* to have it all together doesn't mean they really do. After lengthy discussions with many friends, I have learned that serious troubles and trials can be lurking beneath the façade of a happy, peaceful countenance. And, from time to time, we all have discouraging days and burdens that seem unbearable. We never know when a smile, a wave, a cheerful word, a pat on the back, a touch of a hand, a heartfelt thank you, or a few moments of our time may make all the difference for someone in need.

I have been amazed at how simple service can sometimes be. It takes only a few extra minutes to drop off a plate of cookies or a loaf of bread (if you remember to take them with you), and you don't even need to leave the house to make a phone call. Many years ago, a neighbor phoned me on my birthday to wish me well. The entire phone call lasted no more than two minutes, but I have remembered it for more than fifteen years. I was touched that she would take the time, even though it was really no time at all.

As I passed a complete stranger on the sidewalk years ago, she made a point of mentioning that the peach-colored shirt I was wearing looked good on me. I remember her comment every time I wear that shirt, and I feel good all over again. Just the other day, another stranger told me that she liked my dress as we passed briefly at a convention. There is nothing particularly unusual about the dress. In fact, it wasn't even a dress at all, rather a skirt and a top pulled together in the middle with a belt. But that "dress" will always be special to me now because someone else liked it and took the time to tell me so.

A friend who had recently moved to a new community in another state described how good it made her feel when someone honked and waved to her. She did not know the driver nor did he know her, but that simple, friendly gesture proved to her that someone in the neighborhood was aware of her existence. She knew then that she was not alone in her new surroundings—and she just might grow to like the place!

Because of our inability to do some grand gesture of goodwill, we sometimes fail to do anything at all. Naturally, there will be times when we don't have the time or money to be as kind or as generous as we would like to be, but we must not let that stop us from doing something. The smallest something is certainly better than nothing. It really is the thought that counts. It is nice to know that someone cares—even in the simplest way. The moral to Aesop's fable "The Lion and the Mouse" is that no act of kindness, no matter how small, is ever wasted.

I was reminded of the importance of little acts of kindness when my husband was away on an extended business trip, and I was left alone with eight children. The children had been very cooperative, and I had somehow managed to keep things running fairly well, so I really didn't need any outside help. Nevertheless, despite a house full of people, I found myself feeling lonely. It was quite a responsibility to be completely in charge of all those children day after day with no one to share the burden. How I yearned for another grown-up with whom I could talk. All I needed was a few minutes of adult companionship; but no one seemed to be aware of me. Everyone was preoccupied with their own lives, and I was left to deal with the situation the best I could. One day while indulging in a few moments of self-pity, the thought came to me most forcefully, "Look around—there are many others in your same situation, but they do not have the luxury of knowing their husbands will return in a few weeks as you do. What have you done for the widowed, the divorced, and the lonely that you know?" Immediately self-pity vanished, replaced by guilt—guilt for the people around me that I had ignored, for my own careless insensitivity, for being so preoccupied with my own little world that I had failed to be aware of others. With this newly acquired empathy, I resolved to be more aware of those around me.

In contrast to that situation, my family experienced a great outpouring of compassion by friends and neighbors when I was put on bed rest for a few weeks with our ninth child. We received notes, phone calls, visits, and meals. One family brought us a meal every week until the baby was born—and a few weeks thereafter. In all, they brought a meal every week for at least two months. With a family the size of ours, that is no small undertaking! We certainly didn't need that many meals, and we felt quite undeserving, but it was nice to know that someone cared in such an extraordinary way. Their extra-mile service not only made us feel loved and spoiled, but it also empowered us to endure that challenging time. Whether large or small, kind gestures and acts of goodwill are always appreciated and long remembered.

For many years, I thought of service as a compassionate deed for the person next door, down the street, or around the block. I thought it meant visiting the sick and the lonely, fixing a meal for a needy neighbor, babysitting your sister's children while she goes out of town, volunteering at the hospital, serving on the PTA, teaching Boy Scouts, or coaching soccer. Somehow I had mistakenly thought of caring for my own family as something I was *supposed* to do.

Over the years, however, as my family has grown and I have become increasingly consumed with caring for their needs, service has taken on an added dimension. One day it occurred to me that caring for my own sick children, fixing meals for my own family, teaching and tending my own little ones, volunteering to run them here and there and everywhere, and spending half the night on the couch with my own little baby was every bit an act of service as anything else I might do.

A mother's hands bless her family daily as she performs quiet acts of service in her own home: cooking meals, washing dishes, doing laundry, mending a shirt, mopping a floor, baking a cake, feeding the baby, patting a back, correcting homework, signing papers, giving hugs, holding a hand, caressing a forehead, wiping a tear. Who can measure the impact of these simple acts of service on individual family members?

These daily tasks can be drudgery or delight, depending on my attitude. If I view the tedious, repetitive, sometimes monotonous tasks of homemaking as burdens to be borne or assignments to accomplish, it is easy to become grumpy and irritable as I lose sight of the grander picture. However, when viewing these same tasks as acts of service for the ones

I love most, I can experience the same sense of satisfaction that comes from service outside the home. Notwithstanding all the good that can and should and must be done in the world, we must never become so busy serving others that we neglect the most important people in our lives.

Nobody knows better than you, Mom, how mundane—even oppressive—life can become if you do not find joy and fulfillment in serving others. Attitude is everything! By reaching out to others, we can expand and renew our perspective on life. There is perhaps no better treatment for depression and no better remedy for self-pity. Indeed, service is a potent and powerful tonic that calms the nerves, lifts the spirit, and rejuvenates the soul.

NOTES

1 Lyon, ed., *Best-Loved Poems*, 116.
2 Spencer W. Kimball, "The Abundant Life," 3.

As a Man Soweth

We must not hope to be mowers,
And to gather the ripe gold ears,
Unless we have first been sowers
And watered the furrows with tears.
It is not just as we take it,
This mystical world of ours,
Life's field will yield as we make it
A harvest of thorns or of flowers.

—JOHANN WOLFGANG VON GOETHE[1]

Joy

YOU'LL FIND IT IN THE MOST UNUSUAL PLACES

Weeping may endure for a night, but joy cometh in the morning.

—PSALM 30:5

I was weary and disillusioned as I sat rocking my fussy baby at the end of a long, hectic day when suddenly the thought came to me, "Men are that they might have joy" (2 Nephi 2:25). Surprised and annoyed at the pleasant thought when I was feeling so ornery, I immediately countered, "*This* is NOT joy!" However, as I continued to rock my baby, I found myself wondering, "So what exactly is joy?" As I pondered on its meaning, myriad thoughts paraded through my mind.

Young people see joy as finding their handsome prince or princess and living happily ever after. They view marriage as the end of their struggles and the ultimate source of true happiness. However, they often fail to look past their wedding day and down the road of life to the realities of marriage that involve differences of opinion, compromise, financial obligations, pregnancy, cranky babies, health problems, and teenagers.

One old sage in congratulating a newlywed couple exclaimed, "Well, you're at the end of your problems." Then chuckling to himself, he moved on. What he didn't tell them is which end of their problems they were on—they would discover that soon enough!

As a mother of young children, my idea of joy is having all the children old enough to be potty trained, dress themselves, brush their teeth, butter their own bread, and cut their own meat. But I am constantly admonished by those whose children are older (especially those with teenagers) that "these are the best times of your life, so enjoy them while they're young." I often wonder to myself when I hear their well-meaning advice if there really is any truth in their advice or whether time has dulled their memories of the struggles of these early years. And if, in fact, there is truth in what they say, how can I feel joy at this time of life?

I am reminded of my two young boys who were enjoying freshly baked cinnamon rolls. As they began to eat, seven-year-old Caleb challenged his eleven-year-old brother, "Let's have a race."

Trenton rebuked him gently by saying, "You don't race when you eat cinnamon rolls. You eat them slowly and enjoy them."

Caleb paused momentarily to consider this advice, then cleverly conspired, "I eat mine fast, so I can hurry and get another one!"

Too often I am like Caleb—hurrying through the various stages of my children's lives in the hope that the next one will be a little better. I have even found myself envying those who are single or whose children have left home because they are able to clean the house, straighten the closets, wash the walls and have it stay that way for an entire day. What I fail to remember is that longing and loneliness are often companions to tidiness and tranquility. Instead of wishing my children's young lives away so I can hurry on to something better, I should be savoring the precious time we have together, finding tiny morsels of warmth and sweetness in every day.

If no stage of life is without its trials and challenges, how do we find those morsels of joy on a daily basis in our individual situations? My thoughts returned to my fussing baby. As I rocked him back and forth, I concluded that joy must be something deeper than our outward circumstances and that perhaps it must be experienced *simultaneously* with our trials.

I thought of the early pioneers. They experienced every form of physical deprivation—hunger, thirst, fatigue, cold, heat, and even death—but through it all, they still felt joy. Even at the end of an exhausting day, they were able to sing and dance and praise God with the chorus, "But with joy wend your way."[2] Somehow they were able to see past the challenges of the moment and view life with greater perspective.

My mind then drifted to an experience with my ten-year-old son. His appendix had ruptured, and he needed emergency surgery. Naturally, he was apprehensive, and we were, too. Before the operation, we had a special prayer.

Miraculously, the doctors found that the infection, instead of spreading through his abdominal cavity, had formed a little pocket of tissue that had attached itself to the lining of his abdomen. He ended up with an open wound on the outside of his abdomen into which iodine gauze was stuffed to collect the infection as it drained. This gauze had to be changed morning and evening and was a painful procedure. The whole hospital experience and the days and weeks that followed were emotionally and physically draining as I struggled to care for my young son and my five other children, including a small baby.

However, about a week after our son came home from the hospital, we shared a special, spiritual moment as he told how the prayer that was given before the operation brought him peace and how his subsequent prayers had been answered as he prayed for strength when it was time to change the gauze at the hospital. He had felt warm and peaceful and knew that his prayers had been answered.

As I began to look at this hospital experience from a different perspective, I realized this whole ordeal had been worth it in order to have my son gain a testimony that God lives and that he hears and answers prayers. But it had taken a trial for him to learn this important truth.

Viewed in this light, I saw even more blessings in the trial. First, the miracle that he was alive and the illness had not been more serious; second, skilled and competent doctors knew how to help; third, my son's testimony grew; and fourth, my own understanding and acceptance of God's role increased throughout this experience. The joy was in the trial.

The dictionary defines joy as "the emotion evoked by well-being, success, or good fortune or by the prospect of possessing what one desires . . . a state of happiness or felicity; bliss . . . to experience great pleasure or delight."[3] With this definition of joy, it is easy to understand why we become angry, resentful, or discouraged in the face of trials or adversity.

Oftentimes, we focus so much on the negative in our lives that we fail to notice or be grateful for all that is good. Typically, there is a little bad in the good things that happen to us and usually a little good even in the worst things that happen. How we view the situation can make all the difference.

My neighbor related an incident in which she learned the value of counting your blessings even in a bad situation. While expecting their first baby, she and her husband vacationed in Hawaii. With a late evening flight on the day they were to return home, they decided to do a little snorkeling before going to the airport. However, upon returning to their rental car after an enjoyable swim, they discovered to their horror that they had been robbed! To gain access to the vehicle, the driver's side window had been shattered, enabling the thief to reach in and pop the lever that opened the trunk. Almost everything had been taken—their suitcases, their clothing, their souvenirs, and several rolls of film with pictures of their vacation.

They could have been bitter and angry as they counted their losses, but as they surveyed the damage, they found that there was actually much for which they could be grateful. In his hasty search of the vehicle, the thief had miraculously missed finding her husband's wallet that was tucked under the driver's seat, just inches from the lever that opened the trunk. As a result, her husband had the necessary identification to board the plane. Also, the duffel bag in the front of the car containing their airline tickets and my friend's identification had remained untouched. And for some reason, the thief had not taken a small tote bag in the trunk containing the change of clothes they had planned to wear to the airport. Thus they were spared the embarrassing prospect of going shopping for new clothes in their swimsuits!

After a thorough investigation, they realized they had everything necessary to return home. While they regretted the loss of their personal belongings, including souvenirs and snapshots that would have served as pleasant reminders of their trip, they realized how fortunate they were. They truly had been blessed, and they chose to focus on the positive rather than the negative.

Although there would be no tangible keepsakes from their trip, the loss of their belongings did have its advantages. It certainly made returning home less complicated. They had no cumbersome luggage to haul around, no bags to check at the airline ticket counter, and no waiting in a crowded terminal for baggage at the end of their flight. Furthermore, when they got home, there was nothing to unpack and no daunting pile of laundry to be done. The loss of their clothes also provided the unexpected opportunity to update their wardrobes with a few new outfits. And they couldn't help chuckling to themselves as they imagined the thief's surprise when he discovered that he had stolen a suitcase full of maternity clothes!

Dan Reeves once said, "Difficulties in life are intended to make us better, not bitter." However, we must make a conscious choice to learn and grow from them. I have never forgotten the message I found years ago on a small piece of paper at the bottom of a paper sack while putting groceries away. Apparently it was put there by the young man who was bagging my groceries. It said simply, "What matters most is not what happens to us but in us."

There is purpose in adversity. It can serve to test and strengthen us, leaving us stronger than we were. We can find peace and purpose in life despite our trials. I believe there is much more to our existence than this mortal probation. We are eternal beings. It is my conviction that this life is a test, and the trials we experience are sometimes sent from God to prove our willingness to be obedient in all things and to bring us closer to Him. Knowing this, the trials of life can have deeper meaning than our initial reaction to them.

> Just when all seems to be going right, challenges often come in multiple doses applied simultaneously. When those trials are not consequences of your disobedience, they are evidence that the Lord feels you are prepared to grow more. . . . He therefore gives you experiences that stimulate growth, understanding, and compassion which polish you for your everlasting benefit. To get you from where you are to where He wants you to be requires a lot of stretching, and that generally entails discomfort and pain. . . .

When the Lord closes one important door in your life, He shows His continuing love and compassion by opening many other compensating doors through your exercise of faith. He will place in your path packets of spiritual sunlight to brighten your way. They often come after the trial has been the greatest, as evidence of the compassion and love of an all-knowing Father. . . .

Please learn that as you wrestle with a challenge and feel sadness because of it, you can simultaneously have peace and rejoicing. Yes, pain, disappointment, frustration, and anguish can be temporary scenes played out on the stage of life. Behind them there can be a background of peace and the positive assurance that a loving Father will keep his promises. . . .

As you trust Him, seek and follow His will, you will receive blessings that your finite mind cannot understand here on earth. . . . As you willingly obey . . . you can have the greatest measure of satisfaction in this life. Yes, even times of overpowering happiness.[4]

Mother Teresa summed it up well: "I know the Lord won't give me more than I can handle, I just wish he didn't trust me so much." Despite this knowledge, we sometimes lose sight of the greater purpose behind all that we do. We see our challenges as temporal instead of spiritual. We see them as irritations or interruptions to our plans. God knows us better than we know ourselves. With His help, we can do anything. Trust Him.

As we commit to look for joy in our lives, we will find it. We will begin to catch glimpses of eternity all around us—a sunset, a smile, new-fallen snow, autumn leaves, a rainbow, a song, a kind word, family, friends, an illness, death, and even a cranky baby.

That night as I rocked my little one, I was annoyed because I saw his crying as an interruption to my schedule. I momentarily lost sight of what a blessing it is to be a wife and mother and the privilege I had of rocking and comforting this priceless treasure from God. This challenge, which had been a bother, suddenly became a blessing.

As my baby drifted off to sleep in my arms, I gained a new appreciation for and a new understanding of the purpose of adversity. I had learned an important truth: We can find richness and meaning in life despite our surroundings. That evening I came to know that joy is not something that can be purchased or possessed; it is not necessarily a state of happiness or felicity or bliss or evoked by well-being, success or good fortune, and it is not always a result of great pleasure or delight. Nobody knows better than you, Mom, that true joy may not be the result of our physical surroundings at all. It is a state of mind, not a state of being. Joy is the sweet and peaceful feeling that comes from within when we put our trust in God and know that our actions are in accordance with his will.

NOTES

1 Lyon, ed., *Best-Loved Poems*, 332.

2 "Come, Come Ye Saints," *Hymns of The Church of Jesus Christ of Latter-day Saints* (Salt Lake City: The Church of Jesus Christ of Latter-day Saints, 1998), 30.

3 *Webster's Seventh New Collegiate Dictionary* (Springfield, MA: G. & C. Merriam Co., 1972), 459.

4 Richard G. Scott, "Trust in the Lord," *Ensign*, November 1995, 16–18.

If You Can Smile

If you can smile when things go wrong
And say, "It doesn't matter,"
If you can laugh off care and woe
And trouble makes you fatter;

If you can keep a happy face
When all around are blue—
Then have your head examined, Bud,
There's something wrong with you!

For one thing I've arrived at:
There are no "ands" or "buts";
The guy that's grinning all the time
Must be completely nuts.

—Author Unknown[1]

Humor

THERE WAS AN OLD WOMAN
WHO LIVED IN A SHOE

A merry heart doeth good like a medicine: but a broken spirit drieth the bones.

—PROVERBS 17:22

I was already on edge as I returned from dance lessons with my daughter one Monday evening. We still had dinner to eat, the table to clear, dishes to wash, and a family activity to do before the little ones went to bed at 8:00—and it was already 6:50. Upon entering the driveway, my five-year-old son greeted me at the van, upset about something. When he didn't get a satisfactory solution to his problem, he lay right down on the cement—in full view of all the neighbors—and started bawling. Too uptight to deal with the problem, I walked in the house to get dinner. Immediately my husband started quizzing me about this new dance schedule—was it going to be on Monday *every* week and was it always going to be at *this* time? Too frazzled to discuss it, I simply ignored him. Then I heard bawling outside again. This time it was the two-year-old. Apparently he had fallen out of the wagon as he was being pulled up and down the street by the eleven-year-old. I'm sure all the neighbors enjoyed the delightful dinnertime duo of howling children!

I picked up my still-crying son from the driveway, brought him into the house, and held him on my lap while I tried to eat amidst a whirlwind of activity. The rest of the family had already eaten, so children were darting about clearing the table and clanging dishes. (I had to snatch up my food as it was being hauled away or I would have had no dinner at all.) In addition to all the hubbub, I was trying to comfort a whiney five-year-old while two or three children were eagerly trying to talk to me at the same time—totally oblivious to the fact that I couldn't really hear any of them. I faked a weak smile, nodding and making half-hearted guttural noises from time to time as appropriate.

And then, like the cherry on top of an ice cream sundae, my husband, completely unaware of my frenzied state, poked his head around the corner of the doorway and questioned in his most incredulous voice, "Did you know this CD player has been running since noon?" Exasperated, I silently shouted, *I really don't care!* Instantly, I saw the humor in all the craziness, and the situation passed without escalating further.

If we expect to endure with joy—at least some measure of joy and sanity—we must not take ourselves too seriously. The chaos and confusion of family life can best be handled if it is intermingled with a healthy dose of humor. In the midst of the madness, we sometimes lose control. Tempers flare, and angry words are spoken. The crisis you experience this morning will probably be forgotten by this evening, but sometimes we momentarily forget how relatively insignificant it really is. It is especially easy to become distraught when a sequence of exasperating events occur, creating a raging sea of emotion that finally erupts and boils over, blazing a passionate trail of anger and hurt. We are then left with the arduous task of rebuilding peace and harmony out of the smoldering ash.

Although a series of events can be overwhelming when we're caught in the midst of it, by stepping back for a moment, we can usually see some humor in it. Often situations that seemed overwhelming at the time become hilarious when I relate them to my husband at the end of the day. Comic relief is absolutely essential in enduring and coping with the challenges of motherhood.

I was feeding little Levi one day when he began throwing up. Despite my desperate dash to the bathroom, I wasn't quick enough. He threw up all over himself, the back of the toilet, the toilet seat, the floor, and the sink. After changing the baby, I sat him in the family room while venturing to the bathroom to finish cleaning up. I was upset, and my four-year-old knew it. Instead of his usual chatter and barrage of questions, he followed me quietly from room to room, taking in the entire episode. It wasn't until I almost finished cleaning up that he finally broke the silence. With genuine inquisitiveness, he asked delicately, "Did you have some trouble?"

Trouble?! Sometimes I think that's all motherhood is—a daily succession of one bit of trouble after another. I know exactly how the old woman who lived in a shoe felt. More than once I have been tempted to send my children off to bed with nothing but a dry crust of bread—forget the broth!

How is it that a two-year-old can completely dismantle a room in the time it takes to walk to the garage and throw a diaper away? What possesses children to get into things they know they shouldn't while you're on the phone, and why do they insist on tangling up in the cord while you're trying to speak? How many times has my son wet his pants today? There are wet underpants in the bathtub, on my bathroom floor, and in the boys' bedroom. How did my two-year-old stick a toy in the grill of our van in thirty seconds flat that took me twenty minutes to retrieve? Why do I get indigestion at meal time? (Could it have something to do with the fact that I spend most of the time getting the salt and pepper out of the cupboard, picking up spoons and forks off the floor, taking rolls out of the oven, pouring milk, getting the washcloth for the spilled milk, and then pouring more milk?) How can a four-year-old need to use the bathroom three times during a ninety-minute shopping trip? (I thought only pregnant women had that problem.) Why do they insist on drawing on the wall, on the table, and on themselves instead of on the piece of paper you have provided? Why does the baby always mess his pants right after you've changed him and just before you need to leave? What makes children think you know what to do with everything—dirty tissues, empty candy wrappers, half-eaten sandwiches, and all those special papers from church? With a box full of toys, why do they prefer playing with the pots and pans, the shoes in my closet, the tools from the toolbox, the vacuum attachments, and the cushions on the couch? How is it that two children can turn the bathroom into a flood zone in the few minutes it takes to get pajamas from the bedroom? And, by the way, how does the bathroom get so dirty in less than a day?

Perhaps the most compelling question of all is, "Who is '*I don't know*'?" You know—the guy who sneaks into our homes and breaks dishes, makes messes, cracks windows, destroys priceless heirlooms, scratches furniture, and puts holes in the walls without anyone ever seeing him. Every time I turn around, something is getting broken, ripped, scratched, or soiled. When I ask who did it, my children stand there staring at me with their very best clueless faces. Then one-by-one, they each respond timidly, "I don't know." If I ever get my hands on that guy, he'll be sorry! (By the way, *I don't know*'s brother, *Not me*, lives at my sister's house!)

Clueless and innocent—at least that's what they claim whenever disaster strikes. Yet these very same children somehow manage to find the bag of candy I am saving for Halloween, the chocolate chips I have hidden on the top shelf behind the meat at the back of the freezer, and the marshmallows I have carefully tucked away for the next camping trip. How do they do it?

It is my conviction that children really don't mean to get into trouble—it just comes naturally! Children are born scientists, and the world is their personal laboratory. Our job as parents is to minimize the damage and destruction as they go about their daily business of exploring and experimenting. So much of what they do really does come as a result of their innocence and their innate curiosity. Just remember, it is the scientific side of them that causes them to draw on walls, poke holes in the table with a fork, flush toys down the toilet, hack at your new shrubs with a homemade sword, walk through puddles with new shoes, or roll in the mud created from the irrigation water.

Part of the test of raising children is finding the funny in the frustrating and the humor in the horrible, thereby making the most of the miserable moments. For example, when my young son poured water in the flour bin, I decided that was a good day to make bread. When we went camping and it started to rain during dinner, we could have easily become discouraged. We felt cheated. And like everything around us, our spirits were dampened. Instead, we decided to make the most of an unpleasant situation. Huddling close together in the tent, we sang songs and told stories, and the children still recall fondly that camping trip in the rain when we made the most of a miserable situation.

We don't have good luck when it comes to camping. Nevertheless, I do believe that every family should have the opportunity to build spectacular, love-producing, family-enriching outings while experiencing the thrill of cooperation, companionship, and courtesy. This is best learned while brushing teeth and washing hands out of a two-liter pop-bottle-turned-kitchen-sink, eating outside while holding down paper plates in order to keep the food from being blown away, and then retiring for a peaceful night's sleep on a lumpy hill with ten people crowded together in an eight-man tent!

And so it was with cherished memories such as these that we packed the van for another camping trip—seven children and number eight on the way. This time we had planned something more than the usual trip up the canyon. It was to be a vacation to the Indian cliff dwellings at Mesa Verde in the four corners area of the United States. We had all been anticipating this get-away despite the fact that it would be a long drive in a crowded van—seven hours one way. We arrived just before dinner, set up camp, ate, and went to bed.

The next day we set out early in order to see as much as possible. However, after the first stop, we discovered to our dismay that the van would not start. We had it jump-started and hoped for the best, but after needing another jump-start at the next stop, we knew it wasn't going to be a good day. When the same ranger assisted us the second time, he suggested we go to town and have the van checked. Not wanting to risk another distress call and running out of goodwill with the ranger, we left the van running the rest of the day at each viewpoint. Quickly scanning each site, we then ran back to the van and were again on our way. Needless to say, it was a tense, hurried day, and we were glad when the sightseeing was finally finished. When the van didn't start again the next morning, we decided to cut our trip short and head for home—seven hours back the other way!

The children were grumpy and irritable all the way home, and I can't say that I blame them. To this day, they won't let us forget what a disaster it was, but at least now it is a bittersweet memory and has become a family favorite for a plan gone bad.

Some days are just too much. When things get really chaotic at our house, I often retire to my bedroom to sit in my chair and rock peacefully back and forth while collecting my sanity. It was during one of these rocking/collecting sessions that four-year-old Jarom found me and began questioning, "Mom, are you trying to rexla . . . Are you trying to rela . . . Are you trying to . . ." When he realized he couldn't remember how to say the big word he was trying to say, he finally gave up and said simply, "Mom . . . are you resting?"

"Yes," I replied quietly with all the energy I could muster.

Immediately, he called his three-year-old brother, Abram. As they both ran to me, Jarom repeatedly warned, "Abram, Mom is resting; Abram, Mom is resting." He continued to say this while they both climbed all over me, hugging and kissing. So much for rexla . . . rela . . . resting!

Jarom is our little ball of fire. He keeps our already busy lives even busier. I suppose every family has a Jarom—a comedian, a nonconformist, a bundle of energy bursting at the seams. He's our real live Dennis the Menace. One evening when he was five, he was telling a flannel board story for family night. In the middle of his presentation, he suddenly leaned over to me and whispered something in my ear which I couldn't decipher. Then, unexpectedly, he walked over to Abram, punched him in the stomach, strolled back to the front of the room, and resumed his story as if nothing had happened. We all stared in shock at this seemingly unprovoked action. My guess is that Abram had been doing something annoying, and Jarom's whispered words finally registered: "I'm going to hit Abram." Family life is an incredible test of patience, and sometimes you just have to take a deep breath and roll with the punches!

I keep a journal of the cute antics and clever sayings of the children. Not only is it fun to read, but it is a gentle reminder of their sweet simplicity. Life for them has not yet become fraught with schedules, appointments, commitments, demands, and the complexities of the grown-up world. They are not too busy to become engrossed in watching a bug crawling on the sidewalk, the lineman repairing damaged phone lines, or running water splashing from a spoon in the kitchen sink.

We could all become a little more childlike in this respect. Family life involves so much effort, stress, discouragement, and repetition. We could all use a little down time to help ease the burdens. All work and no play makes mommy a dull person. It's amazing how a few minutes of play can help me refocus.

One of my little boy's favorite games was one we called "Wuller de Wust." The idea came from a poem in a story we read. I counted in the bedroom while they found suitable hiding places throughout the house. As I began to look for them, I chanted, "I'm de Wuller de Wust and you're de ones I'm after. I think I'll skin ya just fer fun; you better run, you better run."[2] When I found a child, he would race away, and we chased round and round the house until I caught and tickled him. It really wasn't much, but they loved it.

In truth, it really doesn't take much—just a little of our time. It can be as simple as a picnic in the backyard, reading a book, making a craft, coloring a picture, hide-and-seek in the house, swinging at the park, or a board game around the kitchen table. Is there anything more engaging or refreshing than the gleeful giggling of a one-year-old or the felicitous frivolity of a two-year-old?

Not long ago, I was either severely hormonally imbalanced or I had a bad case of the grumpies. Either way, it had resulted in several rather dismal days. I felt like I could bite someone's head off in one bite and be perfectly justified in doing so. My husband noticed my testy state and gave a gentle warning that I'd better figure out what was wrong and fix it. How do you fix hormones?

I tried to analyze my situation, but I couldn't put my finger on any one problem. I suppose it was just a nagging, uneasy feeling from having too many unfinished projects that had been dragging out for too long and were starting to wear on me. To make matters worse, it didn't look as though any of the projects would be completed anytime soon. Consequently, I didn't see myself being rid of the grumpies for quite some time either.

Then one evening as I was working in the yard, some of the younger children asked me to join them on the trampoline. I was too grumpy to do anything fun, but seven-year-old Levi pleaded so sincerely that I didn't dare refuse. Holding hands, we jumped in a circle chanting the nursery rhyme, "Ring-a-round the rosies, pocket full of posies, ashes, ashes, we all fall down." Then we fell onto the trampoline, bouncing and laughing.

"'Gain," three-year-old Marissa insisted. And so we did—again and again and again. As we bounced, Marissa kept glancing at me out of the corner of her eye as if to say, "Thanks for jumping, Mom. Are you having fun?" Her eyes sparkled, her mouth was open wide, laughing delightedly. I didn't want it to end.

This is what it's all about, I thought. *The projects can wait, but my children won't.* Before I knew it the children would be grown, and I would have all the time I needed for projects and progress. Besides, would I ever really remember whether the bathroom sink got cleaned today, that the kitchen floor was mopped one day later than I would have liked, or that the painting project was dragging out much longer than anticipated? Is that what I would remember about their childhood? Or would I remember times like this—laughing and jumping happily on the trampoline?

At last, when it started getting dark and a bit chilly, I reluctantly decided we had better go in. The next morning I woke in a much happier mood. The day went better, and that was the end of the grumpies. My problem had been fixed. Maybe it wasn't hormones after all. Maybe it was just a bad case of misplaced priorities.

When all else fails, as it sometimes will, make a little time for yourself—a little laughing, a little jumping, a little bit of serendipity. Do whatever it is that helps you relieve stress and focus more clearly on the real priorities of life—a walk, a nap, a bubble bath, a sunset, or an evening out. My husband realized many years ago the revitalizing effect of our weekly dates, and he gives them top priority. Not only are these dates fantastic for strengthening our marriage, but they also do much for our parenting. We tell our children that by going away for a while, we return better parents. A few hours away from the house and children can do wonders for a mother's emotional and mental psyche.

"Laughter is to life what shock absorbers are to automobiles. It won't take the potholes out of the road, but it sure makes the ride smoother."[3] So kick back, relax, enjoy your children, learn to laugh at yourself and others. Laughter is the key to survival, and nobody needs it more than you, Mom. By catching the fleeting wisps of humor and playful spontaneity in our lives and clinging to them as we would a life raft, we will be better able to combat the tides of tedium and waves of depression that regularly rock the boat in the tumultuous oceans of our lives.

NOTES

1 Lyon, ed., *Best-Loved Poems*, 253.

2 *Walt Disney's America*, "De Wuller-De-Wust," Walt Disney Productions (New York: Golden Press, 1965), 70–73.

3 Barbara Johnson, "Educators Mutual Hope Health Letter," vol. 24, no. 12, p. 7.

The heights of great men reached and kept
Were not attained by sudden flight
But they, while their companions slept,
Were toiling upward in the night

—HENRY WADSWORTH LONGFELLOW[1]

Work

A Synonym for Motherhood

She looketh well to the ways of her household, and eateth not the bread of idleness.

—Proverbs 31:27

*L*et's face it. Motherhood is synonymous with work—darn hard work and lots of it. I am reminded of the trivet my husband's grandmother had hanging in her kitchen: "A man works from sun to sun, but a woman's work is never done." This idea of continual work was characterized unwittingly in the words of my three-year-old son, Caleb, when he asked what I was doing, and I told him I was fixing dinner. "No!" he protested loudly in his young, broken English, "You did fix dinner yesserday!" And so I had . . . and so I was . . . and so it goes, day after day after day—the relentless, never-ending tasks of motherhood.

Not long ago, nine-year-old Abram was scurrying about the kitchen fixing himself some lunch. First, he put some bread in the toaster, and then he got something cooking in the microwave. While the microwave was on, he darted to the fridge, quickly grabbed something out of it, and then dashed back to the microwave before his food was overcooked. Feeling a little crazy, he lamented, "I go here and there and back to here. It would be better if there were two of me!"

I smiled knowingly. How often I have wished the same thing myself. I can't possibly do all the things RIGHT NOW that need to be done RIGHT NOW. I am, after all, only one person. I have heard it said that if the theory of evolution were really true, mothers would have eight arms and two laps.

Over the years, I have learned several things about work. First, work can, is, and should be enjoyable, even therapeutic. "It is only those who do not know how to work that do not love it."[2] Second, work is worthwhile and necessary. Third, children can do much to assist Mother and relieve the burdens placed upon her. Fourth, mothers must set the example and provide the motivation for the rest of the family to work.

I must confess: I like to work. That doesn't mean that I find every project thoroughly thrilling or that I eagerly anticipate all the activities of each day. To be more precise, I should say I relish the sense of satisfaction that comes from the successful completion of a project. I suppose I inherited this from my mother. Her own mother died when she was thirteen, and at that tender age, she assumed most of the homemaking duties for a family of seven. Furthermore, her father was a dairy farmer in upstate New York, requiring the help of the entire family for the success of their business. At an early age, Mom learned the value of a hard day's work. Growing up, I too learned the value of work as I watched her toil from before sunrise until after sunset. She labored nonstop—washing dishes, washing clothes, ironing, sewing, mending, making pies, baking bread, gardening, weeding, canning, cleaning, scrubbing . . . always working.

As a result, I grew up with the vision that motherhood was all about being busy. I usually have some project to work on—a piece of furniture to refinish, a flower arrangement to create, curtains to sew, bread to bake, a bathroom to scrub, or a dirty oven to scour. Some of my happiest days are the days when I mix bread first thing in the morning and get a stew cooking for dinner or when I have a chance to do a big project—anything that provides tangible evidence of my day's labors. (Of course, an hour later no one can even tell it's been cleaned, but at least I know.)

Everything around me can be in chaos, but if a flower bed has been weeded, the oven is glistening, or there is a new flower arrangement on the table, life is good again. It only requires one accomplishment to make the house feel clean again, providing immense satisfaction that carries me through the day, or even several days. I find myself returning again and again to inspect the completed project. A good day's work is so stimulating and rewarding. A task accomplished, a job well done, progress realized—what power, what success, what victory!

Presumably, we all agree that work is worthwhile and necessary. From the beginning of time, man has earned his bread by the sweat of his brow. If no one worked, how would anything get done? Who would drive the trucks that haul away our garbage? Who would grow the food? Who would refine the oil for our vehicles? Who would run the shops and schools and post offices?

On the homefront, who would mow the lawn, clean the house, fix the meals, and do the laundry? It requires the help of each family member to keep things running smoothly, and everyone is happier when the house is in order. I have found that my mind is clearer, my wits more intact, and my patience more controlled when the house is clean.

Long ago, however, I realized I could spend the entire day just picking up after the children and not accomplish anything else, so I came up with a program of selective cleaning—before lunch, before Dad gets home from work, and before bed. By clean, I don't mean immaculate from floor to ceiling (as much as I would like it to be) with shiny ovens, a sparkling fridge, spotless floors, and freshly polished bathroom chrome. I do insist, though, that the beds are made, the clothes are picked up, the clutter is reasonably contained, and the ring around the bathtub is mostly imperceptible.

In spite of our best efforts, there never seems to be enough time for everything. Children can be one of our greatest assets in achieving success in our work. The motto at our house is, "He who works, eats!" It is said in jest, but the message is clear. The children understand that it takes a lot of work to manage a household—especially one as large as ours—and since they live, eat, and sleep here, they must participate in all the tasks necessary to keep things running smoothly.

Children must have a clear understanding about what is expected of them and when it must be completed. They must know that if their tasks are not done well or in a timely fashion, there will be consequences. Consistent, loving enforcement of basic household rules will yield positive results for parent and child.

One key in getting children to work is to limit the distractions— television, computers, and friends. Children must learn that work comes before play. Careful scheduling of playtime with friends can help children make work a priority. What child can concentrate on work when they know their friends are waiting to play, especially when their friends keep saying, "Are you done yet? Can we go now?" By minimizing the distractions, children can more easily focus on the tasks at hand.

On a daily basis, the children at our home are expected to make their beds, pick up their clothes, tidy their room, clean up after meals, do dishes, and help feed the animals. In addition, they have weekly chores such as vacuuming, dusting, mopping, and cleaning bathrooms. They also have seasonal chores such as weeding, shoveling walks, mowing the lawn, raking leaves, gardening, and canning fruits and vegetables. Even small children can be helpful and enjoy feeling useful. In fact, if you can get them working at age two or three—when they are happy to be helpful—it will be easier to keep them working as they grow older.

Children are more capable than we often give them credit for. Do not overlook this remarkable resource. The benefit of their help cannot be overstated. With ten children, I am borderline insane on a daily basis. Quite honestly, my children's help with household tasks is the only thing that has kept me from going over the edge!

Finally, remember, Mom, nobody's better than you at setting an example when it comes to cleanliness and work. You are the motivating force behind what does or does not get done in your home. You must set the standard.

A friend made a keen observation one day when she said, "Any bad habit Mother has will be multiplied by the number of her children." How true it is. If Mom has a habit of dropping her shoes all over the house, chances are, her children will do the same. If you throw your clothes on the floor when you takes them off, it will be hard to convince your children that they should do otherwise. And if you have a habit of neglecting housework or wasting time, it shouldn't be too surprising that your children do the same.

Think how much more could be accomplished if we spent less time at the mall, on the telephone, or in front of the television or computer. Replace idleness with industry—exercise, paint a picture, learn to sew, try a new recipe, write a story, dry some fruit, bake bread, plant flowers, grow a vegetable garden, play the piano, start a hobby, clean a closet, refinish a piece of furniture, or paint a wall. The possibilities are limited only by your own vision and creativity.

Strive each day to complete or make progress towards the completion of at least one project. Set a goal, write a list, get a plan, make a schedule. Organize yourselves and your household. Instead of praying that your burdens will be lighter, pray that your capacity will become greater.

The notion of packing more into a day can be likened to a jar filled to overflowing with small rocks. At first glance, the jar appears to be full. However, a little sand could easily be poured into the jar, filling the gaps and spaces around the rocks. Surely now the jar is full. But not so. A little water could also be added to the jar, filling the unnoticeable space between the tiny grains of sand. Then, at last, the jar would truly be full—but how much more we have added to what we initially thought was a full jar. The pouring of the water, however, must be done cautiously. If done too quickly or in excess, the jar will eventually overflow, making a huge mess.

So it is with life. More often than not, our lives are filled to the brim with activities. We tell ourselves that we couldn't possibly take on one more thing. But, when that one more thing comes along, miraculously, we manage to fit it into our already busy lives. You may have heard it said that if you want something done, ask a busy person to do it. I am sure the busy person has learned that work—like the rocks in the jar—expands to fill the time allotted for its completion. Perhaps the person has learned something about time management, organization, prioritizing, and dovetailing, thus taking advantage of the little gaps of time that occur throughout the day. Perhaps the person has learned something about rising early or working late. Surely they have learned that by working harder, smarter, and faster, they can fill the seemingly insignificant minutes of life with meaningful activities. Time is too precious to waste. Take advantage of the entire day by filling the seemingly insignificant minutes of life with meaningful activities. You will be amazed at the marvelous things you can achieve. Ralph Waldo Emerson said, "Guard well your spare moments. They are like uncut diamonds. Discard them and their value will never be known. Improve them and they will become the brightest gems in a useful life."

But, do not forget that while motherhood is all about juggling a never-ending number of tasks, nobody knows better than you, Mom, that even the best of us can reach a breaking point. We can make a real mess of our lives by trying to go faster or further than we have strength. Be realistic in your expectations. The judicious use of our time and energy must always be our number one consideration in whatever we choose to do.

Notes

1 Lyon, ed., *Best-Loved Poems*, 336.
2 J. H. Patterson quoted by Richard Evans, *Richard Evans' Quote Book*, (Salt Lake City: Publishers Press, 1980), 48.

I Took a Piece of Plastic Clay

I took a piece of plastic clay
And idly fashioned it one day—
And as my fingers pressed it, still
It moved and yielded to my will.

I came again when days were past;
The bit of clay was hard at last.
The form I gave it, still it bore,
And I could change that form no more!

I took a piece of living clay,
And gently fashioned it day by day,
And molded with my power and art
A young child's soft and yielding heart.

I came again when years were gone:
It was a man I looked upon.
He still that early impress bore,
And I could fashion it never more.

Author Unknown[1]

Discipline

TAMING THE WILD CHILD

A wise son maketh a glad father: but a foolish son is the heaviness of his mother.

—PROVERBS 10:1

The first thing cattle do when released into a new pasture is walk the perimeter of the field, checking the fence line. Once they know where the boundaries are, they begin to graze contentedly, feeling safe and secure within the limits set for them. Children also regularly check the fence lines of their lives, testing them for strength and stability. And as much as they may demonstrate otherwise, they really do want sturdy fences which will remain steadfast against resistance and rebellion. Rules and limitations are essential to our children's emotional and psychological well-being. They want to know there are set boundaries that they may not pass without consequence. Then, feeling safe and secure in this knowledge, they can set about the daily business of childhood.

For me, the practice of effective and consistent discipline is one of the hardest aspects of motherhood. While it seems contrary to our nurturing natures, it is nevertheless one of the greatest things we can do for our children. My own tendency is to dismiss a succession of minor infractions of disobedience or quarreling, hoping they will somehow mend themselves—priding myself on my superb use of patience. In reality, each infraction adds kindling to the woodpile which can burst into flames at the slightest provocation. That is not the best way.

Furthermore, repeated warnings become empty threats that children soon learn to disregard if not followed with prompt and appropriate action. By regularly ignoring transgressions, we allow them to become worse. We teach our children that their actions are acceptable, which results in a gradual deterioration of their behavior as they continue to push the limits further and further. If left unchecked, children will eventually break down the fences completely, and they will be left to themselves—aimlessly wandering through life with no clear direction or purpose.

It is much better to confront and correct little problems on a daily basis as they occur. As the mother, we must make difficult decisions and issue timely consequences. Our children will respect us more if one of the many hats worn is that of disciplinarian. We cannot get caught in the trap of relying on our husbands to yield the heavy hand, and we must not pass the buck by saying, "Wait until your father gets home!" It is unfair to Father to always be made out as the bad guy, and the waiting is unfair to the child. The most effective discipline, especially for small children, must occur firmly and consistently. It must occur directly following the offense in order for them to make the necessary connection between the violation and the consequence.

Appropriate discipline can occur without being abusive. We can be strict without striking, punishing without paddling. We can reprimand with restraint and correct with self-control. My husband excels in this area, and I have learned much from watching him calmly yet firmly discipline the children without even raising his voice.

Sometimes when I am insisting that my ten-year-old son do something he really doesn't want to do, he will protest in his very best whiney voice, "Why do I have to?" I often answer him by saying, "Because I love you." Loving our children does not mean always saying yes, giving in, and doing the fun thing. Loving our children sometimes means loving them enough to say no, stand firm, and do the right thing even though it isn't the pleasant or the popular thing.

Henry W. Longfellow said, "The greatest firmness is the greatest mercy." In the short term, it is sometimes easier to choose the path of least resistance. But what consequences will that bring for our children tomorrow? In the long run that decision may not prove to be the most merciful choice. Taking a stand today may actually be the most loving thing you do for your children, although they may not realize it or appreciate it for years to come.

"An infallible way to make your child miserable is to satisfy all his demands."[2] It is true that they're only children once, which is often the reason we give for spoiling them. However, the fact that they are only children once and that childhood is such a relatively small part of their lives is all the more reason to teach, train, and prepare them for life after childhood.

> Parents who have been successful in acquiring more often have a difficult time saying no to the demands of overindulged children. Their children run the risk of not learning important values like hard work, delayed gratification, honesty, and compassion. . . .
>
> Fewer and fewer parents ask their children to do chores around the house because they think they are already overwhelmed by social and academic pressures. But children devoid of responsibilities risk never learning that every individual can be of service and that life has meaning beyond their own happiness. . . .

> The meaning of *more* and *less* is not always crystal clear. There are times when less is in reality more and times when more can be less. For instance, less pursuit of materialism may enable more family togetherness. More indulgence of children may result in less understanding of life's important values. . . .
>
> A . . . conservative approach is the key to successfully living in an affluent society and building the qualities that come from waiting, sharing, saving, working hard, and making do with what we have.[3]

Children today seem to have more of everything—except discipline. On every hand we hear calls for fairness and justice for children. Children's right are heralded to such an extreme that we hesitate to punish for fear of retribution. And while I do not advocate returning to the days of switches and paddles, for our children's sake and for the sake of society, we must be deliberate in the use of discipline on a daily basis.

Unfortunately, discipline has a negative connotation. However, the dictionary defines discipline as "teaching," "learning," "instruction," "training that corrects, molds, or perfects the mental faculties or moral character," and "self-control."[4] Those are not negative characteristics. Certainly punishment is a part of discipline, but only when the rules are broken. Therefore, it behooves us as parents to do our part to adequately teach, instruct, correct, and mold our children so they develop the self-control necessary to behave appropriately.

Like a gardener lovingly pruning and caring for the vines and bushes in his yard, proper discipline means carefully guiding and shaping our young children into the kind of people they have the potential of becoming, rather than allowing them to grow at will—wild, straggly, and out-of-control. It is during their formative years that our children are most easily influenced and most open to direction and advice. Once childhood has passed, it will become more difficult for them to change deep-rooted attitudes and behavior. "As the twig is bent, so the tree is inclined."[5]

Years ago, we had some friends who had planted a pine tree in a spot of their yard where they later realized they did not want it to be. Still, they kept watering and tending it, and it continued to grow. Every spring and every fall they talked of digging up the little tree and moving it to a more desirable location. However, life got the best of them, and before they knew it, the tree was too big to move without causing substantial damage or even death.

Similarly, we must take great care in the planting of our children, for where they are planted, there will they grow. Once their young lives have taken root, it will be very difficult—if not impossible—to transplant and transform their basic personality and character traits. What a terrible tragedy to discover upon reaching maturity—after years of nourishing and nurturing, caring and cultivating—that they had been planted in the wrong spot!

In the vast open spaces of the West, thousands of mustangs thunder across the grassy prairies, running wild and carefree. Although majestically beautiful, elusive, and content—roaming about at will unfettered, untamed, undisciplined—these wild mustangs are of little use to others. Left to themselves, they live and die a self-absorbed existence. However, with significant effort on the part of a dedicated, devoted trainer, they can learn to bridle their wild tendencies, appropriately harness their energy, and bear the burdens of others in meaningful service.

So it is with children. We do them no favors by letting them run through life unbridled. Children, like wild mustangs, achieve their full potential only after patient, persistent, purposeful preparation. They become an asset to society only when their wild, carefree spirits have been carefully corralled. To lovingly build fences of enduring quality is one of the most compassionate endeavors we perform as parents, and nobody does that better than you, Mom.

Notes

1 Lyon, ed., *Best-Loved Poems*, 312.

2 Henry Home quoted by Richard Evans, *Richard Evans' Quote Book*, 18.

3 David H. Burton, "More Holiness Give Me," *Ensign*, November 2004, 98–100.

4 *Webster's Seventh New Collegiate Dictionary* (Springfield, MA: G. & C. Merriam Co., 1972), 237.

5 Gordon B. Hinckley, "Worldwide Leadership Training Meeting" (Salt Lake City: The Church of Jesus Christ of Latter-day Saints, 2003), 21.

BALLAD OF THE TEMPEST

We were crowded in the cabin,
Not a soul would dare to sleep—
It was midnight on the waters,
And a storm was on the deep.

'Tis a fearful thing in winter
To be shattered by the blast,
And to hear the rattling trumpet
Thunder, "Cut away the mast!"

So we shuddered there in silence—
For the stoutest held his breath,
While the hungry sea was roaring
And the breakers talked with death.

As thus we sat in darkness,
Each one busy with his prayers,
"We are lost!" the captain shouted,
As he staggered down the stairs.

But his little daughter whispered,
As she took his icy hand,
"Isn't God upon the ocean,
Just the same as on the land?"

Then we kissed the little maiden,
And we spoke in better cheer,
And we anchored safe in harbor
When the morn was shining clear.

—JAMES THOMAS FIELDS[1]

Prayer

The effectual fervent prayer of a righteous man availeth much.

—JAMES 5:16

My father was very ill, and the prognosis did not look good. The next day, doctors would perform a biopsy to confirm their suspicions. My whole world was collapsing around me. At ten years old, I was lonely and afraid and knew of only one place to turn. In the darkness of my bedroom on that desperate night, I lay in bed pleading, praying, promising.

When the biopsy came back negative, I knew beyond any doubt that God hears and answers prayers—for he had answered mine. I was completely unaware of the many others who had undoubtedly been praying that night also. To me, this was a miracle based solely on the sincere, earnest pleadings of one little girl. That experience has provided a foundation of faith for the years that have followed.

Prayer is the crucial moments of meditation in our otherwise hurried existence when we take time to collect our thoughts, to ponder the purpose and significance of our actions, and to evaluate the direction of our lives. Our prayers should be more than mere ceiling bouncers in which we quickly toss out a few vain repetitions and then go about our business. Our adult prayers should be longer and more meaningful than the first prayer uttered by our two-year-old Caleb: "Heavenly Father, name Jesus Christ Amen." During prayer, it is our privilege to share our concerns, our desires, our hopes, our dreams, our struggles, and our gratitude with a loving Father in Heaven, and it is our blessing to expect answers in return.

> *Prayer is not artful monologue*
> *Of voice uplifted from the sod;*
> *It is Love's tender dialogue*
> *Between the soul and God.*
>
> —JOHN RICHARD MORELAND[2]

My life would be much different without prayer. Many of the decisions I have made were a direct result of answers to prayer. I have sought guidance on all the major decisions of life such as schooling, a career, relocating, marriage, and children. Over the years, however, I have learned that the most powerful source in the universe is also approachable for everyday concerns on a wide variety of subjects ranging from finances to potty training to teaching a child to read. Whether we need a marriage counselor, a child therapist, a psychiatrist, a mentor, or just a friend, God is always there. He can give us the wisdom to know what needs to be changed in our lives, the strength to endure what cannot be changed, and the courage to stand firm in our convictions despite the swirling decadence of the world around us.

When all else fails, pray. Prayer is so private and personal but has such far-reaching results. It is so simplistic yet so vital to our well-being. The impact and importance of prayer in our lives cannot be overstated.

Prayer is my umbrella in the rain, providing shelter and safety during the thunderstorms of life. It is my lighthouse on the hill during long, dark nights of trial and adversity. It stands as a beacon of hope and direction in the blackness that sometimes surrounds me. It is my oasis in the desert. I have tasted the sweet fruit of personal revelation and drunk deeply from eternal wellsprings, providing spiritual rejuvenation as I pause momentarily to bask in the refreshing shade of God's love when this mortal journey drones on like a slow-moving caravan beneath the scorching Sahara sun.

One of my greatest desires is for my children to learn the incredible power and peace that can be theirs through prayer. Even young children can learn this, but it takes effort and commitment. It may take a little extra planning to allow time for morning prayer before everyone scatters in a dozen directions. It means pausing at the beginning of each meal to give thanks and ask a blessing on the food. It means gathering the family together for a final family prayer before retiring for the evening, and then listening at the bedside of the little ones as they learn from experience the value of consistent, personal prayer. It does take effort, but the rewards are worth it.

Children catch on quickly. Do not underestimate their capacity to understand spiritual things. My daughter's religion teacher told an experience of kneeling beside his young son while he said his evening prayer. The little lad was speaking so softly that the father could not hear what his son was saying. Leaning closer, the father gently whispered, "Talk louder; I can't hear you." Without hesitation, the young son opened his eyes, turned towards his father, and said reproachfully, "That's because I'm not talking to you!"

Several years ago while living in Hawaii, we stopped to show some visitors the historic Pali Lookout. It is the site of the last battle of the great King Kamehameha in which he sent hundreds of his opponents plummeting to their deaths from this magnificent mountain peak and was at last victorious in uniting the Hawaiian islands. From this vantage point, one also has an impressive view overlooking Kaneohe Bay and the surrounding communities.

As we climbed out of the van, six-year-old Jarom ran around the far side of the van to get out of the wind; consequently, he did not see us walk up the hill to the lookout point. When he discovered we were gone, he sat down and began to cry. We had been at the lookout about ten minutes before we realized he was missing. Immediately, we rushed back to the van and were relieved to find some tourists waiting with him until we returned.

On the way home, Jarom made his way to the front of our 12-passenger van and whispered to me, "Do you know why you came back so soon, Mom?"

"Why?" I questioned.

"Because I said a prayer."

How grateful I was that even at this young age, he understood the power of prayer. It was a comfort to him that day and will hopefully sustain him through difficult times to come. It is never too early to teach children about prayer. They comprehend more than we think they do.

We must not be afraid to talk of spiritual things with our children. It is by example and experience that they learn. If we want them to learn to read, we spend time reading with them. If we want them to learn mathematics, we spend time helping them add, subtract, multiply, and divide. If we want them to learn to play baseball or basketball, we spend time playing catch or shooting hoops. Likewise, if we want our children to be spiritual, God-fearing people, we must regularly spend time praying with them and sharing spiritual experiences. Abraham Lincoln said, "I remember my mother's prayers and they have always followed me. They have clung to me all my life."[3]

Religion is at the very core of this great country. This nation was founded on religious principles by religious people. Our forbearers sought the guidance of the Almighty in everything they did. Instilling faith in our children today is essential if we hope to continue the rich heritage that is ours.

Years ago, I heard the story of a poor widow struggling to provide the necessities of life for her family. With no worldly goods to bestow on her children on their birthdays, she gave them the only thing she had. With the birthday child at her side, this humble mother knelt in prayer, petitioning God's blessing and protection for her precious child in the coming year. What a marvelous moment. What child would dare stray far having been raised by a mother like that? No accumulation of worldly wealth could compare to the gift of faith her children accumulated year after year while kneeling beside their mother as she shared this prized possession.

In today's world, raising children with strong moral convictions is not an easy task. Unfortunately, children do not come with individual instruction manuals. But in this most important of all earthly pursuits, God will not leave us clueless. As parents, we are privy to the greatest resource of all for raising children—the Creator Himself.

I am so grateful for divine intervention and eternal perspective in this confused and troubled world. I can't imagine struggling through life without guidance from a Supreme Being—someone who loves me unconditionally and is concerned about my personal well-being; someone who is intimately aware of my individual situation and who knows me better than I know myself; and someone who knows the capacity and potential of my children better than I.

Riding my bicycle through the countryside recently, I became aware of the tall, wooden poles lining the street at regular intervals. Phone lines and electrical wires spanned the poles, forming one long strand that stretched for miles. It struck me how amazing it was that here in my little rural community in a rather insignificant part of the world, I could dial a few numbers and be instantaneously connected to cities and towns and places of importance all across this vast nation—or any place in the world.

Even more remarkable is the idea that without any wires at all we can, by our very thoughts, communicate across the universe to the greatest being of all. He, in turn, can respond directly and without delay, providing hope, comfort, guidance, and direction to the daily dilemmas we encounter.

The methods of communication today are staggering. In the midst of a communication revolution, technology is being developed at unprecedented rates. As we become engulfed in the furor of the information age and in our ambition to keep in touch, let us not overlook the most reliable communication of all—prayer. Due to the limitations of man, phone lines become disconnected, computers crash, answering machines malfunction, satellites get disrupted, and emails are lost. But unlike cyberspace where the server is often busy, the heartfelt prayers we send into God's space are always heard and always answered. Even at its best, today's discoveries do not rival the ageless communion between man and Deity in which our very thoughts put us instantaneously in touch with the greatest power in the universe. Thank goodness for prayer—that phone line to eternity, to wisdom beyond our own. And the best part of all is that it's free—every day, all day, holidays included. When it comes to raising decent, honorable, trustworthy children, nobody needs God more than you, Mom. Call home often.

NOTES

1 Lyon, ed., *Best-Loved Poems*, 82.

2 Ibid., 270.

3 Richard Evans, *Richard Evans' Quote Book*, 12.

What God Hath Promised

God hath not promised
Skies always blue,
Flower-strewn pathways
All our lives through;
God hath not promised
Sun without rain,
Joy without sorrow,
Peace without pain.

But God hath promised
Strength for the day,
Rest for the labor,
Light for the way,
Grace for the trials,
Help from above,
Unfailing sympathy,
Undying love.

—Annie Johnson Flint[1]

Guardian Angels

ON WINGS OF LOVE

Make yourself familiar with the angels,
And behold them frequently in spirit;
For without being seen, they are present with you.

—ST. FRANCIS DE SALES

I believe in angels—not the cherubic, picture book kind that float on pillowy clouds of marshmallow white while playing their golden harps and filling the universe with heavenly harmonies. On the contrary, the angels I believe in are much more down-to-earth. They don hard hats and work boots and their hands are gnarled and rough from years of service and wear. Mine are the practical, helpful, get-down-to-business kind of angels.

You've probably come across many of them and not even known it. They are often hard to detect because they look so human. Nevertheless, we've all seen them. In fact, sometimes we find them in our own homes. Many of them live next door, down the street, or across town. We find them bathing and diapering the children after an exhausting day, giving back and neck massages, listening intently, making cheerful phone calls, tending our children while we go out of town, lifting heavy pianos and carrying box after box to the moving van, painting houses and pounding nails, helping with the car pool, sending thank you notes, delivering loaves of bread or plates of cookies, or fixing meals during an illness or after the birth of a new baby. They are husbands, children, parents, friends, and neighbors. They are the real-life guardian angels on whom we lean for strength, love, and encouragement during times of trial. The benefit and blessing of their assistance is invaluable in our lives.

As wonderful as these earthly guardian angels are, however, there will be times when their help is not enough. Sometimes we feel completely alone on this battlefield of life or, at the least, the battle seems terribly lopsided. Notwithstanding this perceived imbalance, it is my conviction that we are never alone. We are part of an army of heavenly hosts. And although our fellow soldiers may not always be visible, they are nevertheless fighting valiantly on our behalf to help us with our daily battles.

One of my favorite scripture stories is one I don't recall hearing until I was an adult. It is a powerful story full of comfort and hope. It is the story of Elisha the prophet and his servant when they were surrounded in the city of Dothan by the king of Syria and his army who were intent on Elisha's capture. When Elisha and his servant realized their predicament, the servant exclaimed, "Alas, my master! How shall we do?" (2 Kings 6:15).

In my mind's eye, I can picture the servant throwing up his hands in despair. They were trapped. Their situation was hopeless. I am sure he felt a surge of emotions at that somber moment—anger, discouragement, and betrayal. There was probably a bit of confusion over the situation and a great deal of fear for the future.

In an effort to comfort his servant, Elisha counseled, "Fear not: for they that be with us are more than they that be with them" (2 Kings 6:16).

A cursory glance of the surrounding landscape certainly revealed otherwise. Undoubtedly, the servant must have wondered about the astuteness of Elisha's statement.

Elisha, seeing with broader perspective, prayed, "Lord, . . . open his eyes, that he may see. And the Lord opened the eyes of the young man; and he saw: and, behold, the mountain was full of horses and chariots of fire round about Elisha" (2 Kings 6:17).

What a remarkable story. Can you imagine the servant's surprise and renewed courage at this amazing discovery? Instead of wrenched, upward thrust hands, I imagine they were reverently clasped, thanking God for divine intervention. He wasn't alone. God would help him.

I have wondered many times if it isn't possible that we too have an army of angels watching over us. And why not? Motherhood is its own kind of battle, often leaving us bruised and beaten with wounds that may not be visible to the naked eye. Some days it seems like we're fighting a one-woman war against overwhelming odds. Still, I suppose the battles we fight as mothers would not always require such drastic measures as an entire army; but it would certainly be comforting to know that we had at least a soldier or two on our side!

One of our more memorable family activities was an object lesson given by my husband. He formed a maze in our backyard by connecting the scattered palm trees with five hundred yards of twine. As he guided each blindfolded person to the starting point, he whispered, "Don't let go." Clutching tightly to the twine, we weaved our way across the lawn, trying to find the end of the maze. Some found it rather easily, while others, much to their chagrin, went round and round the same trees. It seemed like an effort in futility, and we became discouraged, disheartened, and disenchanted with the process. Couldn't we peek just a little?

Couldn't someone steer us in the right direction at the next intersection? Wasn't anybody going to help us? Eventually, though, we all found the end and were greeted by my husband whispering gently, "You made it!"

The children had so much fun the first time that they all wanted to do it again. This time we watched as Jadee and Camille, the last to finish, struggled to find their way. We chuckled silently as Camille made circles around the same trees over and over. With our enlarged perspective, the path was clearly obvious, although to her it was still a maze of confusion and frustration. With my blindfold off, I noticed something else—my daughters thought they were wandering through the blackness alone, but all the while my husband was watching, guarding, and protecting. Often he walked right beside them without them even knowing.

It occurred to me that this experience was not unlike life. While we make our way through this maze of life—groping and searching for purpose and meaning, grappling for answers to our trials and challenges, and grasping for help to meet the demands placed upon us—Father in Heaven stands by, silently and lovingly watching, guarding, and protecting, desperately yearning to hold us in His arms once again and whisper softly, "You made it!" At times you may feel helpless and alone, much like Elisha's servant, when faced with the battles of your own life. Nevertheless, I think we would be amazed and humbled if we knew how aware God is of our personal circumstances and how involved He really is.

Yes, I believe in angels—whether in the form of earthly angels dressed in typical cultural garb or in the form of glorious, radiant, heavenly beings, silent and unseen, on an errand from above. Each renders physical and emotional succor to those with distraught and downcast spirits. God lives. He loves us. He is aware of our individual trials. He can, He will, and He does send help down from heaven in our most desperate hour—especially to you, Mom.

NOTES

1 Lyon, ed., *Best-Loved Poems*, 1.

THE BRAVEST BATTLE

The bravest battle that ever was fought,
Shall I tell you where and when,
On the maps of the world you will find it not;
It was fought by the mothers of men.

Nay, not with cannon or battle shot,
With sword or braver pen;
Nay, not with eloquent word or thought,
From the mouths of wonderful men.

But deep in the woman's walled-up heart—
Of woman that would not yield,
But patiently, silently bore her part—
Lo! There in that battlefield.

No marshaling troop, no bivouac song;
No banners to gleam and wave;
And oh! These battles they last so long—
From babyhood to the grave!

Yet, faithful still as a bridge of stars,
She fights in her walled-up town—
Fights on and on in the endless wars,
Then silent, unseen—goes down.

—JOAQUIN MILLER[1]

Enduring to the End

ONE DIAPER AT A TIME

And so, after he had patiently endured, he obtained the promise.

—HEBREWS 6:15

*I*t won't *always* be like this," I grumble miserably to myself when I'm washing out the third pair of soiled underpants that day, rummaging through the toy box and clothes hampers looking for lost shoes twenty minutes before church starts, dragging five children through the grocery store, or pulling dirty socks and broken pencils out from under the couch.

It's a coping technique I have used over the years to get me through those times when I think I can't take it anymore. It's my way of reminding myself that as difficult as life might be right now, it is not a permanent situation. If I can just hang in there, things will eventually get better.

In my youthful naïveté, I always thought of the elderly in connection with enduring to the end. I thought it meant hanging in there to the end of our lives. I thought it meant finding ways of coping with the illness and pain and loneliness of old age. While these are certainly some of its meanings, I have learned more imminent meanings of the phrase since becoming a mother.

For me, hanging in there means enduring through the night when I pop out of bed so many times I feel like a jack-in-the box. It is on nights like this that I actually look forward to morning so I can stop tormenting myself with the elusive fancy of sleep. Hanging in there may mean enduring to the end of a crying session with a colicky baby . . . rocking . . . patting . . . rubbing . . . walking . . . singing . . . swaying . . . bouncing . . . burping . . . rocking . . . patting . . . rubbing . . . . Enduring to the end sometimes means enduring one more day or perhaps just one more hour. It means one more messy diaper to change; one more child to bathe; one more meal to fix; crayon on the wall; juice on the carpet; gum in the hair; toys down the drainpipe; Legos here, Legos there, Legos, Legos everywhere; dirty dishes, dirty laundry, dirty faces, and dirty footprints across the freshly mopped kitchen floor. It means finding a way to cope with the crying and fussing until all the children are finally in bed for the third time. It is surviving a week of runny noses, croup, diarrhea, throwing up, soccer games, dance practice, choir, basketball, school projects, Cub Scouts, piano lessons, orthodontic appointments, and talks for the children's program at church.

Enduring to the end means enduring the various stages of our lives—pregnancy, nursing babies, preschoolers, a difficult teenager, a college education, unemployment, a painful divorce, a long-term illness, or the death of a loved one. I can't say how many times I've felt like quitting, especially when the end is only a speck on the distant horizon. Too often I feel like a novice trying to run a motherhood course for experts. The course is cluttered with unexpected twists and turns, ascending occasionally at inclines too steep for my experience and expertise. Despite the difficulties of the trail, it is crucial that we have determination to stay the course.

After the birth of our first child, I jokingly said to my husband, "I'll probably be changing diapers for the next fifteen years." While we anticipated a large family, I never imagined how prophetic those words would be. In fact, they fell several years short of reality. Little Marissa finally decided shortly before her third birthday that she was too old for diapers; and before I knew it, she was wearing underpants. For the first time since we brought our first little baby home from the hospital nearly twenty-one years earlier, we did not have one or two children in diapers.

With my first seven children, I used cloth diapers. (If you are a young mother, you may not know what they are, although it is possible you wore them as a baby!) The disadvantage of cloth diapers is that they need to be changed more frequently—approximately every two hours—in order to prevent diaper rash. I have also been blessed with six sons, all of whom have taken much longer to learn the art of toilet training. Some of them have been three years old before making this wonderful discovery. Needless to say, this translates into thousands and thousands of diapers. On rough calculation, I figure I have changed more than seventy thousand diapers—give or take a couple thousand (but who's counting?).

I must admit, it did get discouraging at times; but on the whole, I took great pride in keeping their little bottoms clean and dry. That diaper-changing era seemed like an eternity. It has consumed nearly all of my married life. I have changed enough diapers to fill a warehouse. And while I am still getting used to the idea of life without diapers, I have eagerly looked forward to the completion of this phase of life. Somewhat patiently I endured—one diaper at a time!

While I am complaining, I would like to mention how tired I am of brushing teeth—not my own teeth but the two or three other sets of teeth that I have brushed morning and night, morning and night, morning and night . . . for the past twenty-two years.

Years ago I saw a sign in a dentist's office that said something to this effect: "You don't trust your two-year-old to cross the street by himself, so why do you let him brush his own teeth?" It made sense to me . . . and I've been brushing my little ones' teeth ever since. Looking back now, I believe that that sign was some sort of communist plot to limit the size of our families. After all, who would want to have more than one or two children if they knew they had to brush their teeth morning and night for the first several years of life? And to think that I fell for it!

It wouldn't be so bad if they would stand still and cooperate, but that would make this daily ritual far too easy. First, I have to call them three or four times or hunt them down in some secluded spot in the house. When they see me armed with toothbrush in hand, the chase is on—I'm the enemy! Getting them to the bathroom sink is only half the battle. Once captured, I struggle to pry lips, clenched teeth, and locked jaws apart while holding them in a headlock. Then trying to get the deed over as quickly as possible, I encounter one of two scenarios—either they twist and turn, fuss and fight, scream and squeal, or they clamp down defiantly on the toothbrush, nearly biting it in two. When I finally get in a little brushing and tell them to spit, nothing comes out. What a battle! What should have been a delicate two-minute task has just turned into twenty minutes of torture—for both of us.

Some nights, when I am especially tired and not in the mood for one-on-one combat, I just sit there staring blankly at the crowd of children surrounding the bathroom sink—brushing, flossing, spitting, pushing, and fighting. In vain, I imagine that this is some sort of terrible dream; and any moment I will wake up, and it will all be over.

But that isn't the end of my troubles. There's the hair. We solved this problem with our boys by keeping their hair buzzed short during the warmer months. The problem this creates, however, is that they get out of the habit of combing their hair, and I spend the first two months of winter nagging them to comb their hair every morning. They have even dared to question the necessity of combing their hair for church.

After ten years and four boys in a row, we were blessed with two darling little girls. I was excited about once again doing ribbons and ringlets and braids and bows. My youngest daughter had beautiful golden locks (our own Shirley Temple) which were adorable and elicited all sorts of comments from complete strangers when we took her out—none of whom were in the bathroom with me when I tried combing through the tangled mess. Her hair got so snarled that she became adept at avoiding the hair-combing scene altogether. Some days I chased after her with the comb while she hollered, "No mo', no mo'!" I must confess, some days I compromised by simply pulling her hair up on top of her head—snarls and all—and securing it with a pony tail. (When it was up like that, you couldn't tell the difference between curls and snarls anyway.) I sometimes wondered if we would ever succeed in getting all the snarls out. I figure it will be a few more years before she can comb her own hair. Somehow I hope to endure—one snarl at a time.

Then there's the issue of teenagers! (Do we really want to go there?) We had heard all the horror stories and had received multiple warnings, "Just wait until they're teenagers!" And so it was with anxious dread that we approached our oldest son's thirteenth birthday. But nothing happened. He seemed to glide through the teenage years unaware of the perplexing role he was supposed to be playing. My husband and I looked at each other and said, "What's the big deal?" Then . . . we had more teenagers. And we have now joined with thousands of baffled and befuddled parents for the most tumultuous roller coaster ride of our lives! And you know, the worst part of it is—I hate roller coasters! But it's too late now. The ride has started, and there's no turning back. All I can do is grit my teeth, close my eyes, and hold on until it's over![2]

"Why does it have to be so hard?" I have moaned more than once. "I can't take it any more. It never ends. If I have to deal with one more thumb sucker, change one more set of wet sheets, tie one more shoe, or get one more child in and out of a car seat, I think I'll scream!" I can't tell you how many times I have exceeded the legal limit for stress endured by one mother in one day. There are not adequate words to describe how difficult it gets at times. But I probably don't need any—because you already know. That's the nature of the business we're in.

A few years ago, I was having a particularly bad day. As I left the house to run an errand, one of the children called after me, "When will you be back?"

"Maybe I won't come back!" I hollered sarcastically over my shoulder. "If I'm not home for dinner, just eat without me." Of course, I did come back, but a few minutes away from it all allowed me to clear my head and think more rationally.

Sometimes I do want to run away—far away. It doesn't really matter where—just some place where there aren't any children. Some place where no one cries, fights, fusses, whines, argues, teases, or tattles. Some place where there isn't always someone touching me, tapping me, poking me, pulling on me, climbing on me, calling for me, talking to me . . . always someone needing me. Some place where no one makes messes or loud, obnoxious noises and everyone is always polite and proper.

Children have a knack for turning even the simplest task into something difficult. For example, putting on their coats, getting out the door, and climbing into the van can be a twenty-minute ordeal. More than once lunch has taken half an afternoon—just to fix peanut butter and jelly sandwiches! And there is no such thing as a quick trip to the potty with a three-year-old. Instead of concentrating on the task at hand, they spend their time talking about the roll of toilet paper, the light switch, the color of their buttons, the new pair of panties they are wearing, the smudge of jelly on their shirt, and the spider in the corner of the room. By the time they finish inspecting their little cubicle, they have forgotten the main purpose for the visit—and it is probably too late anyway. (Now you get to do clean up.)

In today's world, a large family is a bit of a novelty—eliciting a variety of reactions from people when they discover how many children we have. Thankfully, most of the comments have been positive and complimentary, one of the most common being, "Oh, you must have a lot of patience." Are you kidding? I stand there staring at them—mouth gaping open, deciding whether to laugh or cry or shake them sadistically. I can't tell you how many times I have warned my children, "I'm running out of patience!" Too often my nerves are stretched to the breaking point and beyond. Each additional child has steadily depleted my supply of patience until the little bit I did have has long since been used up. What might be perceived by outsiders as patience is really a sort of numb, robotic survival mode I went into shortly after baby number three.

Developing patience with a large family is analogous to putting a frog in a pot of boiling water. If you drop the frog in when the water is already boiling, he will immediately hop right back out. However, if you put him in a pot of cool water and gradually increase the temperature, he doesn't even notice that he is being slowly cooked to death.

Likewise, if I had been given ten children to care for twenty years ago, I would have lost my mind immediately. But, by having them one by one over an eighteen year span, I have gone insane a little at a time.

Patience is an acquired virtue, and I believe God sends children to help us acquire it. Judging by the number of my children, it is obvious that I am a slow learner, but it hasn't all been in vain. With each child, my ability to do and be and endure has enlarged. As my family has grown, so has my capacity. In no way do I claim to have mastered the art of patience, but I have definitely become better at faking it!

Sometimes I reflect on the days when we had three or four children and how overwhelmed I felt. Today I recall those good old days fondly, and smile inwardly as I think to myself, "If only I had known then what I know now." Today with a houseful of children, I often feel as though I have reached the limit of my capacity, and, still, I wonder if in some future day these times will also become the good old days. What more will yet be required of me? How much more stretching will I have to endure? I know that I am more patient, more capable, more grateful, and more empathetic today than I was a few years ago. Things I once found distressing hardly faze me now. The trials of the past have helped to mold and mellow me.

I had an interesting experience years ago with my oldest son who was then just three years old. We had gone to the park, and while there, we saw a young boy—perhaps ten or eleven years old—riding a bicycle. As I pointed to the boy, I said to my son, "See that little boy over there." After looking around in confusion for several seconds, my son said, "You mean that *big* boy?"

In that brief interaction, I learned something that has stayed with me over the years. Only one boy was riding a bicycle, but to one of us he was little and to the other he was big. It's amazing how perspective can shape our views of the world around us, and I have often contemplated how biased my view of a situation may be because of my individual circumstances. I view the world much differently today as a mother of many children than I did when I was a child or as a teenager. And I am sure my outlook on motherhood will be different when the children are grown and gone. And then I have wondered, could this varied perspective also apply to other challenges in life? Would they take on a completely different meaning if viewed from another perspective?

Not long after the birth of our tenth child, we attended a family reunion. With children ranging in age from five months to eighteen years, life had escalated to such a hectic pace that much of the time I was completely overwhelmed by it. My husband's aunt who had raised eight children asked me how things were going. "Fine," I lied, rolling my eyes and trying to fake a smile. Quite honestly, it was just too much effort to explain the sickening, panicky feeling I had much of the time—like someone who had been riding a whirling merry-go-round far too long, going way too fast, desperately wishing the ride would end. Even if I had tried to explain how things really were, it probably would have come out in a gush of mumbled, disjointed thoughts—the mere mention of which would have elicited a flood of tears that were hiding just below the surface.

I am sure she saw through the façade, and at that moment there were many things she could have said. She could have launched into a sermon on the merits of motherhood, offered up a few trite words of encouragement, or condescendingly sympathized with my plight—none of which would have been consoling or appreciated. Instead, she said something totally unexpected. Simply and sincerely, she counseled, "This too shall pass." Spoken with sympathy by one who knew, those four little words had a more profound effect on me than anything else she might have said.

In fact, her words touched me so deeply that I couldn't keep back the tears when I repeated them to my husband later.

This too shall pass? I wouldn't always have a throng of children clamoring for my attention? I wouldn't always have that nagging feeling that I was forgetting to do something important? And I wouldn't always feel like a walking zombie—being forced to function on less sleep than medically prudent? This crazed, overwhelmed, helpless, out-of-control, fatigued feeling would eventually pass? I had, it seemed, been caring for babies forever, and, so it seemed, I would continue to do so forever. I had become so consumed with the here and now that I had failed to notice any tomorrow. As difficult as it was to imagine—someday, somewhere, somehow—I would be a normal personal again.

This too shall pass. Along with the passing of these difficult days would be the passing of many of my most precious moments—my children's laughing faces, dancing eyes, and tiny sing-song voices. Although the days and weeks sometimes seemed to drag on endlessly, in retrospect, their childhood would be over in the blink of an eye. I needed to capture all the goodness of this brief and fleeting phase of life, focusing more on the merriment and laughter, the sweetness and innocence.

That knowledge sustained me through the stressful months and years that followed as I struggled to raise my children, including a baby who was in no hurry to grow up. I felt strengthened, encouraged, and empowered to go on. Those days of diapers, binkies, and bottles are behind me now, but I have learned much about perseverance, patience, and endurance in the process of it all. There is great satisfaction in sticking with a difficult task and seeing it through to completion. The ensuing sense of achievement is worth the effort.

Perfection is a long, hard journey with many pitfalls. It's not attainable overnight. Eternal vigilance is the price of victory. Eternal vigilance is required in the subduing of enemies and in becoming the master of our lives. It cannot be accomplished in little spurts and disconnected efforts. There must be constant and valiant, purposeful living. . . .

The real tragedy is the tragedy of a man who never in his life braces himself for his one supreme effort, who never stretches to his full capacity, never stands up to his full stature. To lie down and moan and whine about limited opportunities is the part of weaklings. To grasp the opportunities at hand and walk forward is the way of the strong."[3]

Although life can seem unfair at times, we must not give in to hopelessness or despair. Enduring means finding ways to cope and persevere in spite of the difficulties we may encounter, pushing forward with hope and optimism. Enduring to the end certainly includes a lifetime, but when all is said and done, the ultimate test and measure of our success is how well we endure the trials that come to us weekly, daily, even hourly.

Enduring does not mean woefully existing in a world void of happiness. Rather, enduring means to continue living—happy, meaningful living. While the road of life may be full of ruts, you don't need to get stuck in one. You will enjoy the journey more if you don't get tripped up on every pothole. Learn to step nonchalantly over and around them. You can choose to brood over every bump and crevice in the road, or you can enjoy the wildflowers blooming along the way. In large measure, you will take from life exactly what you choose to take depending on your perception of the world around you. While the journey may seem long and difficult, but nobody's better than you, Mom, at finding snippets of joy and wonder along the way because you know that it won't *always* be like this.

Notes

1 Lyon, ed., *Best-Loved Poems*, 223–24.

2 Debbie Bowen, *W.O.R.K.: Wonderful Opportunities for Raising Responsible Kids* (Springville, UT: Horizon, 2004), 83.

3 Spencer W. Kimball, "The Abundant Life," 6.

The Hand that Rocks the Cradle
Is the Hand that Rules the World

They say that man is mighty,
He governs land and sea;
He wields a mighty scepter
O'er lesser powers that be;
But a mightier power and stronger
Man from his throne has hurled;
For the hand that rocks the cradle
Is the hand that rules the world. . . .

Blessing on the hand of women!
Angels guard its strength and grace,
In the palace, cottage, hovel,
Oh, no matter where the place;
Would that never storms assailed it,
Rainbows ever gently curled;
For the hand that rocks the cradle
Is the hand that rules the world.

Woman how divine your mission
Here upon our natal sod!
Keep, oh, keep the young heart open
Always to the breath of God!
All true trophies of the ages
Are from mother-love impearled;
For the hand that rocks the cradle
Is the hand that rules the world.

—William Ross Wallace[1]

Enjoying the Journey

STEPPING OVER THE POTHOLES OF LIFE

Be a joyful mother of children.

—PSALM 113:9

With the birth of my seventh child came a deeper understanding of this concept of enjoying our enduring. This baby was so challenging that I questioned the existence of justice in enduring such a miserable, grumpy, colicky baby. When he was just two months old, I longed for the day he would turn one and—I hoped—be a little easier to manage. However, that first birthday may as well have been an eternity away when every day seemed like a year. I soon took on a survival mentality, planning each day to accomplish only those tasks that were absolutely crucial, leaving limitless unfinished details to another day. After all, I reasoned, they too will eventually come to the top of the critical list and, at that point, I would tackle those projects.

The baby became an all-consuming project not only for myself but also for the entire family. When I couldn't calm him, I passed him to my husband or one of the children so I could get some work done. They would then pass him to another . . . and another . . . and so on until all of us had had a turn, and then we started over. In fact, it got so bad that instead of arguing over who *got* to hold the baby, the children would argue over who *didn't have to* hold the baby. This little guy literally cried through dinner every night for the first six months of life. We began eating in shifts just so we could enjoy a meal. My sanity hung by a thread for most of that first year. I felt like the picture of a cat clinging by its claws to a tree branch with the caption: "Hang in there, baby."

Despite the difficulties, it was during one of his crying spells that I came to appreciate what it really means to be a mother. First, I tried feeding him. When he wouldn't eat, I tried burping, then rocking, then feeding, then burping. Finally after an hour and a half of nonstop crying and this vicious cycle that seemed to be going nowhere, I too began weeping bitter tears of despair. Completely overwhelmed and exhausted, I desperately yearned to be anywhere, doing anything besides sitting on the couch enduring my baby's relentless crying.

I thought of friends and family members who were not married but longed to have a family, and I speculated angrily, *If only they could see me now, they would be grateful they didn't have any children.* No sooner had this thought entered my mind than a flood of cherished memories enveloped me—memories of the good times with my children, memories that made me glad I was a mother. However, in my near-delirious state, I also felt the intense and bitter pain that sometimes accompanies motherhood. In my mind's eye, I had a conversation with a single friend who had never had children. I discussed the burdens of motherhood while she gently reminded me of the blessings that accompany this difficult journey.

Although the story that follows is only an imaginary conversation with a faceless person while I sat crying on the couch trying to comfort my colicky baby, it was a turning point for me as I struggled to put my role as mother into perspective. It is a summary of all I have been trying to convey. In short, it is my testimony of the extraordinary mission of motherhood and the beauty and magnificence of it all—an understanding that has come to me steadily and simultaneously while I have been preoccupied with the sometimes menial and mundane tasks of mothering.

***

In her tailored suit, she watched me as I struggled with my flock of little children. It had been a long, hectic day. There were errands to run, and there had been fighting and fussing and feedings in the car. And now, as we waited in the lobby, two were relieving tension by wrestling and teasing; one was fussing for a drink, and I tried to calm him while I bounced the baby on my knee; the toddler ran back and forth exploring all the newness of the room, while an older child followed close behind to prevent any damage; still another sat engrossed in a novel, oblivious to the commotion going on around her. I was tired and frustrated and felt so conspicuous in the room that was otherwise quiet.

As I looked at the well-groomed woman across from me, I became painfully aware of my own tattered condition. My hair was pulled up in a simple pony tail, and I was wearing faded jeans and a T-shirt that the baby had spit up on three times that day.

I noticed the woman's eyes focus first on one child and then another and back to me again. Suddenly I recognized her. She was well-known and respected in the community, and I knew that she was single. I thought perhaps she was irritated with our interruption into her stillness. But at last she spoke, and I detected a longing in her voice, "What a lovely family. You are so fortunate to have so many children."

Catching me in a moment of weakness, I replied sarcastically, "Would you like to take a few?"

"Surely you don't mean that!" she exclaimed. "To have a child is the most wonderful gift of all the gifts of God. You see, I have never married or had any children of my own, and I envy those who are so richly blessed. I have never felt that first flutter of new life within me. I have never watched my stomach rise and fall as a little leg or arm moved across my abdomen. I have never heard the rhythmic beating as the doctor listened to the baby's heartbeat or seen images of its tiny body on an ultrasound screen."

"Well," I retorted, "let me assure you, there's a lot more to nine months of pregnancy than little flutters and the rise and fall of your abdomen. The excitement of pregnancy is soon overshadowed by the misery of waking up sick morning after endless morning. I cannot begin to describe the awful feelings of morning sickness—the voracious appetite, the endless nausea, the incredible fatigue. Ironically, while my stomach may be churning and nothing sounds appetizing, some foods cause cravings so strong they're almost an obsession. And, if the nausea weren't enough, I feel so lethargic. It's not uncommon to want a nap in the early morning and then again at noon, and still retire early in the evening. Then, shortly after the morning sickness leaves, I begin to feel so big that even the smallest chores such as tying my shoes, taking a bath, or simply walking down the hall become an overwhelming burden."

She readily acknowledged that while pregnancy probably wasn't enjoyable, it was God's way of sending His precious spirits to earth. "Perhaps, too," she mused, "it is His way of helping us appreciate them just a little more." And then, almost in a whisper, she added, "I yearn for a baby more than anything. I yearn to hear that first cry as it is welcomed to this world; to smell that fresh, newborn smell; to feel the velvety softness of its skin; to look into its innocent, trusting eyes and wrap its tiny hand around my finger. I yearn to hold its delicate, fragile body in my arms and know that it is my very own."

Understandingly, I admitted that there was something truly sacred about the birth of a baby and those first precious moments of life. And I had to confess that giving birth is so incredibly marvelous that all the pain and discomfort of the previous nine months are swallowed up in the beauty of the moment.

"However," I added, "birth brings with it a whole new set of challenges. Despite the sweetness of the newborn baby, they are extremely demanding. There are sleepless nights filled with diaper changing, feeding, and rocking and days when the cries of the newborn seem to blend into one continual cry. Sometimes I awake feeling so exhausted that I wonder how I can possibly make it through another day. My body begs for rest, but somehow I force it to continue . . . just one more hour . . . one more day.

"And even when the baby is sleeping, there isn't time to rest because there are other little faces looking to me for love, help, and attention. There are quarrels to quell, bruises to bandage, and hearts to heal. With a houseful of children, there is always a steady drone of busyness and semi-organized chaos. My dream of an immaculate, peaceful home has long since vanished, only to return in some distant day when all the children are grown.

"Because of this continual clutter and constant cleaning, there is little time to pursue a career, a hobby, or a talent. And, here again, I have resigned myself to the reality that many of those things will have to wait for another day. In fact, there is barely time to read or ponder or even pray. The demands upon me are overwhelming, and I have precious little time to call my own. Often, I have so many chores to accomplish at once that I feel as if I am in a funnel spinning round and round being pulled by some incredible force beyond my control."

"Yes," she said thoughtfully, "I'm sure life is demanding. On the other hand, I come home to an empty house every night. Sometimes, for me, the silence is so thick it is almost stifling. While you have so much of commotion and chaos, I have too much of silence and solitude. Sometimes the minutes seem to pass like hours while the ticking of the clock echoes through the house like a siren in the night.

"There are never any little faces looking to me for love and help and attention. There are no smiles of recognition from a newborn baby, no sounds of children's laughter, or tiny voices calling 'Mama.' There are no memories of sleepovers, birthday parties, or the excitement of Christmas morning. There are no children to love and care for me in my old age, and there will be no grandchildren to hug and spoil and gleefully shout 'Grandma.'"

When she finished speaking, we each sat silently for a moment, contemplating our separate situations. Her life had been one of self-fulfillment, success, and opportunity. She had time to continue her education, travel, and study. She was well-known in her chosen profession and had received the praise and recognition of many. Her resume boasted many honors, accomplishments, and awards. She had done much good and performed much service to benefit mankind. Many had been blessed because of her efforts, and the world was a better place because of her.

My world, on the other hand, was limited to the four walls of my own home. I realized that while I may never have time to pursue all my goals and may never be known outside my small sphere of influence, and while motherhood was demanding, frustrating, and tedious, it was worth the sacrifice. A day full of stress could be wiped away with a single slobbery kiss, the happy gurgling of a little baby, two chubby arms around my neck, or a sweet "I love you" accompanied by a bouquet of dandelions.

And, just as this woman received monetary rewards and public recognition for her efforts, motherhood too had its paydays—those first awkward steps attempted by a new toddler; the sparkle in a little child's eyes when they learn to write their name, read a book, or ride a bicycle; a piano recital; a soccer game; college graduation; marriage.

Suddenly there dawned in each of us a new understanding—we had different missions in life. Mine was to raise children in righteousness and help them become capable, competent, contributing members of society, thus passing on to the generations that follow a heritage of intellect, industry, and integrity. For a time, some of my goals and ambitions in life would be put on hold while I pursued this career called motherhood. At that instant, I caught a glimpse of time as God sees it and realized how quickly the children would be gone, and I would be left with only memories of their childhood and the time we had spent together. I knew then that motherhood was worth any sacrifice.

She had another mission. Perhaps hers couldn't be accomplished if her days were filled with diapers and dishes and the demands of caring for a family. For a time, a brief moment in God's time, she would pursue another career. She would find happiness and meaning in life by reaching out to those around her. Through service, she would make the world a better place for many of God's children.

And so we parted, each a little wistful at the advantages and blessings of the other, yet, at the same time, more determined to be grateful for the mission God had given us and to fulfill it with greater resolve and renewed commitment.

***

You will find more joy in the motherhood journey when you truly come to know that nobody's better than you, Mom!

Notes

1 Lyon, ed., *Best-Loved Poems*, 219.

Two Temples

A builder builded a temple,
He wrought it with grace and skill;
Pillars and groins and arches
All fashioned to work his will.
Men said, as they saw its beauty,
"It shall never know decay;
Great is thy skill, O builder!
Thy fame shall endure for aye."

A mother builded a temple
With loving and infinite care,
Planning each arch with patience,
Laying each stone with prayer.
None praised her unceasing efforts,
None knew of her wondrous plan,
For the temple the mother builded
Was unseen by the eyes of man.

Gone is the builder's temple,
Crumpled into the dust;
Low lies each stately pillar,
Food for consuming rust.
But the temple the mother builded
Will last while the ages roll,
For that beautiful unseen temple
Was a child's immortal soul.

HATTIE VOSE HALL[1]

Being There

THE ULTIMATE SACRIFICE

As is the mother, so is her daughter.

—EZEKIEL 16:44

Years ago, I gave up my dream job to become a wife and mother. Immediately following college, I had secured employment with Eastern Airline's reservations center in Salt Lake City. It was perfect—eight to five, Monday through Friday, with all the benefits.

I had always been fascinated with airports—the hustle and bustle of people coming and going; bags and boxes and bundles being heaved and hauled and handled; pilots and flight attendants strutting briskly in their sharp-looking uniforms. As a young girl, I dreamed of one day being part of this grand and exciting business. I too would fly to far away places on fast-moving planes. Now at last I had my chance. Dreams sometimes do come true, and I was living mine!

However, it did not last long. A year later when I married, I quit my job to live near the university where my husband was finishing his undergraduate studies. While I felt some sadness at leaving a job I really enjoyed and one that had been so short-lived, the decision was not difficult. As much as I had dreamed of traveling to exotic, exciting places, my greater dream and number one priority in life was to become a wife and mother.

By our first anniversary, we were blessed with a beautiful baby boy. While we were delighted with our growing family, we were also very aware of our precarious financial situation. With my husband now pursuing an intense graduate program, money was tight. The limited income he brought in was not meeting our needs. I worked at several odd jobs from home, hoping to make enough money to support us. However, as the months passed, we found ourselves regularly dipping into our small savings account, and it soon became apparent that it would not sustain us much longer. After much deliberation, it was decided I would go to work for a time in order to provide the necessities of life.

Reluctantly, I began the search. I was fortunate to find work which allowed great flexibility in the hours I worked—four hours a day, five days a week. The situation was as ideal as possible under the circumstances. We were also fortunate to find a friend who was willing to tend our son. I rationalized that it was good for my child to socialize with the babysitter's two little boys who were close to his age, although I knew intuitively that a few hours of occasional casual play was different than being left in another's care on a daily basis.

A year later when our daughter was born, it became even harder to leave my children. I was able to cut back my work week to three days, doing some of the work from home. Still, passing off my precious newborn to another while I went back to work was one of the hardest things I have ever done. My maternal instincts rebelled at the prospect, and everything inside me wished it could be otherwise. I cried all the way to work, yearning for the day when I could once again be a full-time mom.

These were *my* children. I *needed* to be there. I *wanted* to be there. I wanted them to learn *my* values and beliefs. I wanted to cuddle with them when they woke in the morning instead of starting the day at a hurried, hectic pace—rushing them out the door after a quick breakfast. I wanted to kiss their owies and wipe away their tears. I wanted to watch them play, read them stories, and answer their questions. I wanted to share in all of their growing up time. After all, that is why I had become a mother.

However, as much as I regretted being away from my children, I soon realized that work also had rewards. I was able to have intelligent, adult conversations during the day with sentences longer than three or four words. Those for whom I worked expressed genuine praise for the tasks I performed, and I received monetary rewards and raises for my efforts. Furthermore, no one at work smeared sticky jelly on my desk, tugged at the phone cord while I spoke, puked on my shoulder, or scribbled on my important papers. In fact, no one even touched my important papers. I could arrange them neatly on my desk before leaving one day, and they would be just as I had left them when I returned the next day. Amazing!

Not quite two years after I began working, my husband accepted an internship as part of his schooling, enabling me to be home full-time with the children. While I was delighted with the idea of being home, I suddenly realized how much my self-esteem and personal worth had become connected with the workplace. At work I got immediate thanks and recognition for a job well done. My efforts were acknowledged and appreciated.

On my last day of work, I could barely make my way out of the building for the tears that clouded my vision. They spilled over in the parking lot and ran down my face all the way home. What was wrong with me? Isn't this what I had longed for? Why wasn't I happy? In the days immediately following, I found myself feeling lonely, confused, and frustrated.

At home, I was often taken for granted by the little ones who were completely dependent on me and completely unaware of my sacrifices in their behalf. The children didn't praise me for the fabulous breakfast I fixed or the timely, nutritious lunch I provided. They didn't ooh and ahh over the great way I cleaned the tub and toilet or how well I organized their toys. They didn't thank me for brushing their teeth or doing the laundry. There were no bonuses for nighttime feedings and 2 A.M. sheet changings when they lost last night's dinner all over their beds. And no one complimented me on how smartly dressed I was in my blue jeans and sweatshirt.

I did the same repetitive chores day after day. No matter how hard I worked today, it wouldn't lighten the load for tomorrow. Tomorrow I would do them all again.

There was certainly an adjustment period. Nevertheless, I learned to find joy in what I did, not because anyone noticed, but because it was my privilege to do it. I found great contentment and fulfillment in caring for my children and making our home a pleasant place to be. I enjoyed expanding and refining my homemaking skills and learning to manage our home so it ran efficiently—at least most of the time.

Being home, however, meant that our income had been reduced. My husband was still going to school and working to support us, and we struggled to make ends meet. Those college years were certainly not easy. They were emotionally and financially draining. When my husband finally earned his doctoral degree (after nine seemingly endless years), we had five children and were living proof that you could have a family and go to school at the same time. It was definitely a struggle, but we learned that with faith and hard work it could be done.

We learned to make do on a limited budget. I can remember when our total monthly income was a mere five hundred dollars. Even today it seems like a miracle that we survived on such a meager amount, but somehow we did. We learned to do without a lot of material things. Our children wore hand-me-downs, and I shopped at thrift stores. I watched the grocery store ads, bought food on sale, and made meals from scratch. We drove used cars and owned little furniture. We ate out once a year—usually on my birthday—and even then we went to restaurants that offered free meals to the birthday person. While many of our peers were buying homes, new cars, and expensive play toys, we were paying for textbooks and college tuition. Sometimes we wondered if we would ever finish school or own a home, but we eventually did both.

My attitude towards motherhood would not be the same today if it had not been for the trials and challenges of those early years. In retrospect, I am deeply grateful for them. They were a refiner's fire—a painful one to be sure—but I would not trade them for any financial security or comforts we may have otherwise had. Those trials have been the building blocks that have shaped and strengthened my commitment towards motherhood. I have come to know that motherhood truly is a partnership with God, and He will bless us spiritually, physically, and temporally as we earnestly seek His help and guidance. When I look back on it now, I realize that while we were pursuing a secular education, we were also gaining a spiritual education as we were taught valuable lessons from the Lord's school of life. Our faith was tested, but, like a muscle that is being exercised, we have grown stronger from the stretching.

Those college days are behind us now—thank goodness! But the faith and sacrifice of raising a family still continues. Today my husband has a good, steady income which, thankfully, has increased substantially since those early years. Still, looking down the road of life, we see many years of orthodontics and very lo-o-ong grocery lists. Sometimes we wonder how we'll manage to provide for ten children—not to mention six hungry boys, four of whom will be teenagers at the same time!

Some time ago I heard a radio advertisement claiming that it costs $170,000 to raise a child—Wow!—no small chunk of change. But isn't sacrifice what parenthood is all about? We knew going into it that there would be sacrifices. Parenthood means spending our own hard-earned dollars to buy food and clothing for someone else. It means giving up some of our wants and maybe even our needs to pay for music lessons, soccer shoes, dance outfits, basketball camps, and medical treatments. It may mean driving old cars, wearing worn clothes, and having used furniture in order to provide for those in our charge.

And the sacrifice is not only financial. With the birth of each new child, I wonder how I will find the time, patience, and energy to care for them. With so many children, I have learned to put many of my own ambitions on hold while I nurture my children. On a daily basis, I yearn to do other things—sew curtains, read a book, clean a closet, write a story, or simply take a nap. There are not enough hours in a day to meet the needs of my children and pursue all of my own interests. I have come to the realization that there is a time and season for all things. While my children are young, this is the season to enjoy and nurture them. There will be other days for other things. If I invest my time wisely now, the Golden Years will indeed be golden as I develop long-neglected interests or venture down partially explored, overgrown paths while reaping a rich and plentiful harvest and enjoying the fruits of years of toil and sacrifice.

Do not misunderstand. Parenthood does not mean the sacrifice of all things. Our own mental and physical well-being should be a top priority, and we must regularly schedule time for something we find personally rewarding and fulfilling—without feeling guilty about it. You cannot give from an empty cup. But the reality of raising babies means that most of our days—and often our nights—will be spent caring for them.

As much as we may wish it were otherwise, we cannot do it all—at least not at the same time. Something has to give. The terrible sensation of being pulled in too many directions is not a pleasant feeling. Anything worthwhile requires sacrifice—a college degree, an Olympic medal, musical proficiency, or artistic talent. Each accomplishment requires the sacrifice of other things. Motherhood too requires sacrifice. Perhaps it will require the sacrifice of personal goals, dreams, and ambitions in order to devote our greatest time and energy to raising our children.

That is what motherhood is all about—establishing priorities and then giving those priorities our greatest time, effort, and commitment. Today the role of mother is becoming even more complex. As mothers are pulled in so many directions, it is easy to relinquish our primary responsibility as caregiver and nurturer to others. How ironic that we sometimes neglect the very thing that qualifies us to be mothers.

No more sacred word exists in secular or holy writ than that of *mother*. There is no more noble work than that of a good and God-fearing mother. . . .

She who can paint a masterpiece or write a book that will influence millions deserves the admiration and the plaudits of mankind; but she who rears successfully a family of healthy, beautiful sons and daughters, whose influence will be felt through generations to come . . . deserves the highest honor that man can give, and the choicest blessings of God.

A child needs a mother more than all the things money can buy. Spending time with your children is the greatest gift of all.

When you have fully complemented your husband in home life

and borne the children, growing up full of faith, integrity, responsibility, and goodness, then you have achieved your accomplishment supreme. [2]

Being a mother means "being there" for our children. Be there for them before school, after school, when they go to bed, before a date, and after a date—even when they're late! Just having you there is sometimes enough. Play with them. Do things with them—camping, hiking, outings, vacations, picnics, a trip to the library, games in the backyard, a movie in the evening.

Even teenagers need Mom to be there—although they might never admit it. If I am going to be gone when my children get home from school, my seventeen-year old son will remark regretfully, "So-o-o . . . you'll be gone when we get home?" And the first thing I hear my teenagers wonder out loud when they get home and I am not readily available is, "Where's Mom?" Sometimes I wonder if teenagers don't need Mom even more than younger children. At this confusing and troubling stage of life, teens need someone who can offer the stability and reassurance for which they are so desperately searching. The pressure on today's teenagers is incredible. There is so much that is ugly and degrading in today's world. Hence, the need is all the greater for the consistent influence of mothers to teach, love, inspire, and motivate. We need to be there to take advantage of those rare teaching moments as they occur.

While waiting in a dentist office recently, I read an article about a popular actress and her decision to be home with her teenage daughter. She had strict criteria about the kind of films she would do—only movies of a family nature shot near her home, and no filming during summer vacation. As a result, she doesn't get a lot of work, but she is perfectly happy with her decision. She summed it up this way: "I'm the mommy in my house, and I want to be the mommy in my house. My not being in the house leaves a really gaping hole. All the work built my fame and certainly made me more money, but the toll it took in my home was not good."[3]

Like billboards along the highway, life is full of distractions—work, careers, committees, appointments, meetings, cooking, cleaning, gardening, chauffeuring, and shopping. Too much of our time and energy is spent in the pursuit of worldly wealth—homes, vehicles, furniture, clothing, jewelry, campers, trailers, boats, and large stock portfolios. Contrary to popular opinion, however, all the wealth and recognition of the world is nothing compared with the treasures of family.

Too often we spend "quality" time with our children in an effort to assuage our feelings of guilt over not spending quantity time with them. But a day at the water park, however memorable, cannot compensate for endless days of coming home to an empty house and not having Mother there to wipe a tear, give a hug, or lend an ear. Think what we could do to the rate of crime and delinquency if Mom were more accessible. How much more easily we could shape our children's characters if we spent more time reading, playing, and teaching values instead of pursuing activities of far less consequence.

Going on a walk is one of my family's favorite Sunday afternoon activities. It was during one of these walks years ago that we discovered that by holding hands and stretching out our arms, we could fill up the entire road. Looking at my family stretching from roadside to roadside, it suddenly occurred to me what an awesome responsibility it was to be a mother. I found myself questioning my mothering abilities and the impact I was having on my children's lives. As we walked hand-in-hand down the street, I realized how symbolic that afternoon walk was to our mortal journey. Our role as mothers is to provide strength and encouragement for our families as they trudge down the treacherous road of life.

To a large extent, much of what happens inside our homes today will be the way it is done in our children's homes tomorrow and in their children's homes after that. In a literal sense, we who are mothers have a great opportunity to direct the future of our posterity and our nation by shaping the children in our care today. It is not a responsibility to be assumed lightly, half-heartedly, or part-time. While much that is good and worthy and important is done in the office and the boardrooms and the capitol buildings, in reality, it is in the home that the future of our nation is determined.

Former First Lady Barbara Bush pointed this out years ago:

> Whatever the era, whatever the times, one thing will never change: Fathers and mothers, if you have children, they must come first. You must read to your children and you must hug your children and you must love your children. Your success as a family, our success as a society, depends not on what happens in the White House but on what happens inside your house.[4]

In our daily dilemmas and doldrums, we must never lose sight of the grand purpose of motherhood. It is an awesome responsibility. Sure, it is taxing and tiring and tedious, but it is not easy shaping children's lives, who in turn will do the same for their children . . . and their children . . . and their children. Motherhood is all about leaving a legacy that will span the ages. It is humbling to be part of such a glorious and sacred undertaking.

It has been my blessing and privilege to be a stay-at-home mom for most of my child-rearing years. I realize that in today's world I am one of the rare and the fortunate. I also realize that there are some who desperately long to be home with their children but cannot. I am well acquainted with those feelings of internal turmoil and the tugging of the maternal heartstrings. May you be comforted in your silent yearnings. If you could be home, may you consider the possibility of doing so. I can think of nothing more rewarding or worthwhile than to love and nurture and teach my own precious children. However, this opportunity did not come accidentally or without sacrifice.

I have not seen nearly as much of the world as I had dreamed, nor have I lived the glittery, glamorous lifestyle I had envisioned—traveling by jet to remote parts of the world, visiting museums and sites of profound scientific or historical interest. In fact, I haven't done much traveling at all. Most of the trips I have taken have been to the grocery store, to the doctor's office, and to the potty with two-year-olds. While my dream job was brief and fleeting and brought some measure of personal achievement, my greater dream of being a wife and mother has been all that I had hoped—and more. It has brought great challenge but even greater fulfillment. I have found peace and contentment in just being a mother.

Being home has been its own kind of excitement. In addition to fast-moving planes, I have found other forms of transportation to be equally exciting—stroller rides, training wheels, and teenage drivers! I have learned much about life and human nature in trips to the park, picnics in the backyard, and walks around the block. I have traveled by proxy to nearly every part of the world while reading aloud to my children. Together, we have found adventure and amusement in our virtual travels.

Over the years, I have come to realize what an honored position I hold as mother. Mother not only means nurse, cook, housekeeper, and laundress. It also means confidant, counselor, comforter, protector, guardian, storyteller, teacher, exemplar, and friend. I have been the sounding board for grand inventions, casual conversation, and deep philosophical insights. I have answered hundreds of questions over the years and kissed an equal number of owies. I have enjoyed snuggling with my little ones in the morning instead of throwing on their clothes, stuffing breakfast down their throats, and rushing them out the door. I have enjoyed cradling them in my arms, singing lullabies, and watching them drift off to sleep at nap time. And I have enjoyed being there when they got up again.

One of my greatest pleasures in life is wrapping my children in my arms for a few minutes of leisurely snuggling when they wake. No matter what I'm doing, I scoop them up in my arms for a little bit of cuddling. Some days it lasts only a few minutes before they are distracted by other things. On other days we cuddle and cuddle, neither of us wanting it to end. I can guarantee there is no babysitter in the world who loves snuggling with my children as much as I do.

I admit there have been times—especially on those hectic days when everyone is crying and cranky and I'm on the verge of going crazy—when I've been enticed by the thought of some quiet beach on some deserted island in some far off place. But I can honestly say that if I knew years ago what I know now, I would do it all over again.

I know I am not alone in my decision. Every day millions of mothers around the world make similar sacrifices for their children. They sacrifice their own needs for the needs of their children. Why do they do it? Because they know that, as Freda Ingle Briggs said, "there will always be worthwhile causes, but not always a two-year-old in your lap." Quite simply, they know that childhood does not last forever.

While the role of motherhood receives little public recognition or social prestige, and it is not a job for which you get paid in tangible green cash, it does have rewards all its own. Make no mistake about it—motherhood is the greatest job you will ever do. You need never feel inferior or make apologies or excuses for choosing to be a mother—especially a stay-at-home mom. There is nothing more gratifying than being the most significant person in a child's life, but it is an honor that does not come without price.

Again I am reminded of my little boy with the dart gun and the Lincoln Logs. I believe he voiced aloud the silent wish of every child when he puckered up his lips and pouted, "I wanted you to be there." Have you ever tried to calm another mother's baby? It just doesn't work. When times are the worst, a child wants his own mother. As inexperienced or incompetent as you may feel as a mother, you can still do it better than anyone else, simply because "you're the one."

So, as we make our way along the road of life, searching and stumbling, wandering occasionally down alluring paths of beguiling worldly enchantment, let us clasp hands and cling ever more tightly to our families—the only tangible possession of lasting significance and the most precious of all positions or possessions. May our investments of time, talents, and money be for that which provides lasting joy and bears eternal consequences. As mothers, may we have the courage, the commitment, and the conviction to be there for our children. Because, after all, "Nobody in the wh-o-o-ole world is better than you. *Nobody's* better than you, Mom!"

Notes

1 Lyon, ed., *Best-Loved Poems*, 224–25.

2 Ezra Taft Benson, "To the Mothers in Zion," 1–2.

3 Meg Grant quoting Jamie Lee Curtis, "Starring as Herself," *Reader's Digest*, Dec. 2004, 97.

4 James E. Faust, "A Thousand Threads of Love," *Ensign*, Oct. 2005, 4.